When Life Meets the Soul

We will never understand everything that happens in our lives. Some people turn away from God when they sense that He has treated them unfairly. The wiser choice is to run to God; with our frustration and pain. We need His presence more than we need answers. *When Life Meets the Soul* gives practical insights needed when we walk through the "dark nights of the soul."

—**Gary Chapman**, PhD, *New York Times* bestselling
author of *The 5 Love Languages*

Dr. Parke knows about life—about its heartaches, hardships, and hallelujahs. He also knows his Bible. One of his closest biblical friends—a subject of many years of study—is the patriarch Job, who encountered incredible suffering. In a series of easy-to-read chapters, Dr. Parke brings Job's lessons right into our situations. Open the cover of *When Life Meets the Soul,* and you'll be drawn into a world of encouragement that comes from the heart of Scripture.

—**Robert J. Morgan**, pastor and author

Any student of the Bible is quite familiar with Job, his foibles of suffering, strangely permitted by God, his patience and faithfulness and ultimate blessing. However, any attempt to study this lengthy treatise bogs down in the philosophical diatribes of Job and his friends. Bible scholar Ivan Parke has analyzed, sifted the narrative and dialogues, and provided a delightful understanding of the Book of Job. It is not an exposition but is not lacking in enlightened theological insights. Supported by an abundance of cross-referenced passages of Scripture, literary sources and personal illustrations, *When Life Meets the Soul* will bless the reader with unexpected practical applications to cope with the common challenges of life and faithfully live for the glory of God.

—**Jerry Rankin**, president emeritus,
International Mission Board, SBC

In *When Life Meets the Soul*, Dr. Ivan Parke strikes a unique balance between reading the Book of Job as a scholar and reading it as a simple disciple. I found myself regularly appreciating the expository insights he offers, and I also felt deeply touched by the practical wisdom he shares. Dr. Parke is at once a compassionate counselor offering pertinent encouragement to the hurting, and at the same time a faithful professor providing interpretive guidelines for understanding one of the most thought-provoking books in the Bible. Whether you're looking for a better understanding of the Old Testament, looking to deepen your theology of suffering, or searching for some answers in your struggle, this book is a gem waiting to be excavated!

—Shawn Parker, PhD, executive director,
Mississippi Baptist Convention Board

Parke delivers abundant comfort to those who are wrestling with the indignities of life on this side of eternity. Part pastoral, part personal, and thoroughly framed by careful scholarship, *When Life Meets the Soul* presents us a viewpoint on Job that may be termed, incongruously enough, delightful. Parke deals squarely with the pain and suffering depicted in Job but constantly beats a hopeful refrain that God loves us, God has a plan for us, and in the end, we can delight in the knowledge that God is trustworthy.

—Gene C. Fant Jr., president and professor of English,
North Greenville University

Sufferers take heart. *When Life Meets the Soul* can help you see God's faithfulness amidst our darkest hours. Parke's book is timely as depression and suffering seem to be at an all-time high. Lessons from Job stand the test of time.

—Angela Correll, award-winning author of
Grounded, Guarded, and *Granted*

Suffering is real. God is real. For many, those truths are irreconcilable. For others, those truths are reconciled by the judgment of God upon the sin of man. Or perhaps, there is yet another way to understand this problem. And to that end, Ivan Parke in his book *When Life Meets the Soul* has served us all beautifully and wisely in this consideration of the Book of Job. You will be stretched and blessed and comforted in your own journey while becoming equipped to be a better friend than these who counseled Job. You will be greatly helped through this book!

—**Greg Belser**, DMin, pastor, Morrison Heights
Baptist Church (Clinton, MS)

If you have experienced suffering or tragedy in your life, then *When Life Meets the Soul* is for you. Ivan Parke pulls out the truths found in the book of Job and applies them to our lives so that we can handle the suffering that comes our way.

—**Philip Gunn**, Speaker, Mississippi House of Representatives

Part Bible commentary; part personal journal; and part discussion of what it means to be a divine image-bearer. In *When Life Meets the Soul*, Dr. Ivan Parke provides all of those and more. With the insight of a biblical scholar and the compassion of a pastor, Dr. Parke pulls back the curtain of the ancient world of Job, the people who surrounded him, and the God who permitted calamity in the life of one who deserved better—or so it would seem. Read *When Life Meets the Soul* to better understand the activity of God that can only be seen through the eyes of faith.

—**Les Hughes**, PhD, pastor, author and
cofounder of EntrePastors

Ivan Parke writes as he lives: as a wise, erudite, and loving family man, professor, and friend. Blessed and stressed as any human being with both joys and sorrows, pleasures and pains, he offers *When Life Meets the Soul: Everyday Lessons from the Book of Job* at the intersections of the rich, mysterious, and ancient biblical book of Job, of Job's human life, and of ours. Individual readers who approach each chapter thoughtfully, focusing initially on the chapter titles and then allowing the Father, thought, and time to bring to light insights from Scripture can come away with expanded perspectives and practices as they confront life with a spiritual mindset and faith in God.

—**Rhoda Royce**, former editor, LifeWay Christian Resources

This timely book *When Life Meets the Soul*, by my friend Ivan Parke, is a jewel that will not be hidden long. I cannot imagine ever studying this Old Testament character without this invaluable resource by my side. With the keen mind of the scholar, he is, and heart of a shepherd that exudes from deep within him, Dr. Parke addresses lessons from Job that many people have never noticed. I even found myself wanting to bow in worship, at times, while reading various paragraphs. This book will be a constant companion for my future storms. I will likely reference numerous sections from this work when communicating from Job for the rest of my days. I commend it to you with absolutely no reservations. None.

—**Hal Kitchings**, DMin, pastor and author of *Next Verse*

Professor Ivan Parke has added to the commentary on the Book of Job in *When Life Meets the Soul*. Job, which I have been reading of late, is an under-consulted book on righteousness, suffering, and faith. Parke gives Christians rich examples of the ways in which most of Job's friends' attestations resemble the flimsy theologies of our day. They insist that the favor of God is guaranteed if there is obedience. Truth is, we know better. We have all known saints, like the author's late mother, who experienced the harshest of realities on this side of eternity. The reader, especially one who has faithfully served the Lord and given credit to God for provisions, can find comfort in these everyday lessons from Job. The message of Job is ultimate redemption, and that in our human frailty, we must realize as St. Paul implored, "We see but a foggy image, then we shall see face to face."

—**Joseph Odenwald**, EdD, president of
Southwestern Michigan College

In this excellent book *When Life Meets the Soul,* Ivan Parke has provided a compelling introduction to the book of Job that not only mines the riches of the biblical text, but also invites the reader to ponder how timely the lessons of Job are for the everyday experiences of our contemporary life. Blending compelling illustrations, clear exposition, and relevant application, Parke has gifted the church with a work that is valuable for the teacher, pastor, small group leader, and lay-leader alike to take, read, and live to the glory of God.

—**David Eldredge**, PhD, pastor of Dawson
Memorial Baptist Church (Birmingham, AL)

In *When Life Meets the Soul* Ivan Parke takes the wisdom of Job and translates it into wisdom for the twenty-first century. Parke's work provides a thoughtful, theological, and practical approach to the question of "How should I live?" This helpful and delightful read is great for those looking for insight into the book of Job as well as practical wisdom in living the Christian life.

—**W. Madison Grace II**, PhD, associate professor of Theology,
Southwestern Baptist Theological Seminary

The title of this study of the life of a man named Job is a strong indicator of the encounter that awaits the reader—a rich soul-filling experience. As a scholar, Ivan Parke draws from his depth of collected knowledge and breadth of a lifetime of learning to introduce us to the seemingly unlimited lessons we can learn from the life of Job. As a pastor, Ivan shepherds us through the challenging realities of living lives of purpose through the pleasure, pain, and everything in between. As a teacher, he acknowledges and poses questions that may very well launch a lifetime of essential study and reflection. As a human being, Ivan joins us a fellow traveler on the Godward journey of soul-filling discovery. Whoever walks through the pages of *When Life Meets the Soul* will be blessed by each page and compelled to continue their quest by opening the Holy Scriptures to see the source of this study in the ancient but so relevant story of Job.

—**Rob Futral**, PhD, field shepherd with Standing Stone
Ministries and founder of Paraklesis Ministries

WHEN
LIFE
MEETS THE
SOUL

Everyday Lessons from the Book of Job

Ivan D. Parke

NASHVILLE

NEW YORK • LONDON • MELBOURNE • VANCOUVER

When Life Meets the Soul

Everyday Lessons from the Book of Job

Published in New York, New York, by Entrepastors Press, an imprint of Morgan James Publishing. Morgan James is a trademark of Morgan James, LLC.
www.MorganJamesPublishing.com

Proudly distributed by Ingram Publisher Services.

Morgan James BOGO™

A **FREE** ebook edition is available for you or a friend with the purchase of this print book.

_____

CLEARLY SIGN YOUR NAME ABOVE

Instructions to claim your free ebook edition:
1. Visit MorganJamesBOGO.com
2. Sign your name CLEARLY in the space above
3. Complete the form and submit a photo of this entire page
4. You or your friend can download the ebook to your preferred device

ISBN 9781631958892 paperback
ISBN 9781631958908 ebook
Library of Congress Control Number:
2022931985

Cover Design by:
Christopher Kirk
www.GFSstudio.com

Interior Design by:
Chris Treccani
www.3dogcreative.net

Builds with... **Habitat for Humanity** Peninsula and Greater Williamsburg

Morgan James is a proud partner of Habitat for Humanity Peninsula and Greater Williamsburg. Partners in building since 2006.

Get involved today! Visit MorganJamesPublishing.com/giving-back

To Joya Parke

(1940-2010)

Mom's trials ended at age seventy when, according to Old Testament scholars, Job's began. She handled her suffering like a follower of Jesus. Though atop the ash heap, she prayed for all of us.

Contents

Illustrations

The Tie That Binds

September 11. It was a Saturday in 1993. That evening, I hastily drove my expectant wife to Woman's Hospital in Baton Rouge. Her contractions were five minutes apart. Two hours later, Anne Marie, our first child, entered this world.

September 11, eight years later, was a blissful Tuesday in Mississippi. It looked like a great day for our daughter's party until planes crashed into buildings. Thousands of people died. A war on terror began.

How does one reconcile a birthday celebration and a national tragedy on the same day? *C'est la vie.* The answer is life, not necessarily the answer we want to hear.

Birth and death define life. Its highs and lows connect us all.

Allow me to introduce myself. As of this writing, I am fifty-seven years old; an Asian Indian, born in Bombay, and a naturalized American since 1974; presently a professor at a Baptist college in Mississippi, formerly a pastor; a husband for thirty-two years and a father of two children.

Although we have not met face-to-face, I know two facts about us.

xxii | **When Life Meets the Soul**

Fact #1: You and I are a lot alike.
Fact #2: You and I are unique.

Four similarities illustrate the *first fact*.

1. Living, Not Inanimate

   The mass of the earth, including its contents, is 6 x 10^{21} metric tons. Living organisms weigh 8 x 10^{12} metric tons, just 0.0000000013 percent of the earth's mass.[1]

2. Human Being (*Homo sapiens*)

   According to taxonomists, as many as ten million species of living organisms share the planet with us.[2]

3. Needs

   Mr. Elliott, my world history teacher, informed our tenth-grade class that mankind has five basic needs: food and water, clothing, shelter, security, and religion.

4. Purpose

   Colossians 1:16 states: "For by him all things were created, in heaven and on earth, visible and invisible, whether thrones or dominions or rulers or authorities—*all things were created through him and for him*" (ESV, italics mine). In other words, we were created for God. Genesis 1:28 states, "Be fruitful and multiply, and fill the earth, and subdue it; and rule over the fish of the sea and over the birds of the sky, and over every living thing that moves on the earth." God created everything else for us. Five imperatives define our importance: "be fruitful," "multiply," "fill," "subdue," and "rule."

Twelve differences illustrate the *second fact*.

1. Heredity
2. Experiences or Memories
3. Appearance
4. Personality
5. Relationships
6. Possessions
7. Opportunities
8. Deeds
9. Beliefs
10. Preferences
11. Aversions
12. Goals

Each similarity is a tie that binds: "Birds of a feather flock together." Each difference intensifies our magnetism: "Opposites attract." Each difference also increases our relevance, the ability to relate to a variety of peoples.

About Job and about Us

The Old Testament introduces us to the patriarch Job. Although we cannot meet him face-to-face, two facts characterize Job and us.

> The adjective "patriarch" places Job in the same era as Abraham, Isaac, and Jacob, a period recorded in Genesis 12-50.

Fact #1: All of us are a lot alike.
Fact #2: Each of us is unique.

Job, I concede, seems more unlike us than like us.

There was a man in the land of Uz, whose name was Job, and that man was blameless, upright, fearing God, and turning away from evil. And seven sons and three daughters were born to him. His possessions also were 7,000 sheep, 3,000 camels, 500 yoke of oxen, 500 female donkeys, and very many servants; and that man was the greatest of all the men of the east. (Job 1:1–3)

And the Lord said to Satan, "Have you considered my servant Job? For there is no one like him on the earth, a blameless and upright man, fearing God and turning away from evil." (1:8)

Now when Job's three friends heard of all this adversity that had come upon him, they came each one from his own place, Eliphaz the Temanite, Bildad the Shuhite, and Zophar the Naamathite. . . And when they lifted up their eyes at a distance, and did not recognize him, they raised their voices and wept. . . Then they sat down on the ground with him for seven days and seven nights with no one speaking a word to him, for they saw that his pain was very great. (2:11–13)

And the Lord restored the fortunes of Job when he prayed for his friends. . . and the Lord blessed the latter days of Job more than his beginning, and he had 14,000 sheep, and 6,000 camels, and 1,000 yoke of oxen, and 1,000 female donkeys. And he had seven sons and three daughters. And in all the land no women were found so fair as Job's daughters. And after this Job lived 140 years, and saw his sons, and his grandsons, four generations. And Job died, an old man and full of days. (42:10, 12–13, 15–17)

In the preceding passages, notice the superlatives: wealthiest, most righteous, worst suffering. Jill Briscoe reflected, "Job packed an awful lot of living and an awful lot of dying into his life. He lived a full life. It was full of joy and full of sorrow, full of peace and full of turmoil. It was full of desires realized and plans frustrated."[3]

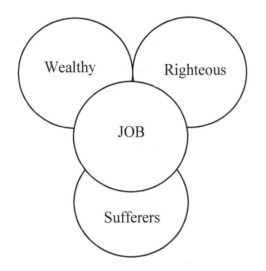

Job Links Three Groups of People

One common denominator, however, counterbalances Job's extremes: life. American poet and philosopher George Santayana asserted, "*Life* is not a spectacle or a feast: it is a predicament."[4] Danish philosopher Sören Kierkegaard noted, "*Life* can only be understood backwards; but it must be lived forwards."[5] Thomas La Mance complained, "*Life* is what happens to us while we are making other plans."[6] Indian Prime Minister Jawaharlal Nehru explained, "*Life* is like a game of cards. The hand that is dealt you represents determinism; the way you play it is free will."[7]

Like us, Job was not born with a silver spoon in his mouth. He declared, "Naked I came from my mother's womb, and naked I shall return there" (1:21). One fateful day wiped out the assets that years of labor had produced. No possession, insured or uninsured, is secure (Matthew 6:19; John 10:10).

Like us, Job was not born righteous. He chose to obey God (Job 31). Prosperity and adversity tested that commitment.

Like us, Job was born bound by space and time. He could not foresee the tragedies that would overwhelm him. He could not stop the long-term suffering that followed (Job 3; 30). He could not escape (7:11–21; 14:13; 29:1–25). He could not control life.

About How to Live

Contrary to common notions, the book of Job addresses more than suffering and teaches more than patience (i.e., "rainy day" lessons). Its content encompasses the essence of life, integrating the best of times and the worst of times. Accordingly, *When Life Meets the Soul* contains responses, twenty-four in all, to a universal concern: "How should I live?"

On mountaintops or through valleys, to live well is to walk with God. No exceptions. In *your* life, is spiritual intimacy a memory, a reality, or a goal? I invite you to encounter God in the book of Job. He's waiting for us.

1

Give Me *You:*
Being Personal

Why do experts invent complicated terms for ordinary phenomena already having an established, easier-to-pronounce name? Case in point, "motherese." According to developmental psychologists, motherese is "a simplified, redundant, and highly grammatical form of language employed by parents in communicating with their infants."[8] A.k.a. "baby talk."

Before our young son Jonathan learned to talk nonstop, I would speak to him in an atypical manner (i.e., higher pitch and unconventional enunciation). A.k.a. motherese. Whenever I picked up Jonathan, he would hear one of *my* vintage statements: "Give me *you!*"

The Priority of Relationship

Atop an ash heap, Job cried out, "Give me *you!*"

1

Chapters 1–3, 6–7, 9–10, 12–14, 16–17, 19, 21, 23–24, 26–27, 29–31, 40, and 42 record Job's utterances. Read them carefully. He never prayed for healing. He longed for his wealth just once (29:1–6). He craved relationship throughout the story.

Anyone who withholds kindness from a friend forsakes the fear of the Almighty. But my brothers are as undependable as intermittent streams . . . Have I ever said, "Give something on my behalf, pay a ransom for me from your wealth, deliver me from the hand of the enemy, rescue me from the clutches of the ruthless"? (6:14–15, 22–23 NIV)

God has made my brothers my enemies, and my friends have become strangers. My relatives have gone away, and my friends have forgotten me. My guests and my female servants treat me like a stranger; they look at me as if I were a foreigner. I call for my servant, but he does not answer, even when I beg him with my own mouth. My wife can't stand my breath, and my own family dislikes me. Even the little boys hate me and talk about me when I leave. All my close friends hate me; even those I love have turned against me. (19:13–19 NCV)

I cry to you for help and you do not answer me; I stand, and you only look at me. I go about darkened, but not by the sun; I stand up in the assembly and cry for help. I am a brother of jackals and a companion of ostriches. (30:20, 28–29 ESV)

Who, Not What

Did anyone offer himself or herself to Job? His wife did not. She advised Job, "Curse God and die!" (2:9)—her last words in the story. His friends did not. They hollered doctrine. His family did not. They avoided him until God blessed him twofold (42:10–11).

Between tragedy and recovery, Job endured a torrent of words until God's self-disclosure: two lengthy speeches from the whirlwind (38:1–40:2; 40:6–41:34). God revealed *Himself*; specifically, His roles as creator and caretaker. He never mentioned Job's woes. He did not counsel Job.

Whenever adversity strikes friends or family, why do we ask "what" questions?

What should I say?
What should I do?

Whenever adversity strikes friends or family, they ask "who" questions.

Who will come to me? I am lonely.
Who will listen to me? I cannot be silent.

In the 1982 bestseller *Megatrends: Ten New Directions Transforming Our Lives*, John Naisbitt divulged, "Whenever new technology is introduced into society, there must be a counterbalancing human response—that is, *high touch*—or the technology is rejected."[9] Therefore, an ATM cannot replace a bank teller. Voice mail, e-mail, fax, text, or tweet will not eliminate the phone call, appointment, or meeting.[10] Pressing "0" needs to be an option to bypass the modern labyrinth affectionately dubbed the Automated Voice Answering System. If customers prefer a personal touch, would not sufferers also?

Civil war during the 1990s devastated Somaliland. Hundreds of thousands of its citizens died as a result of injury, disease, or starvation. Nik Ripken oversaw a humanitarian effort to alleviate the great suffering. In his book *The Insanity of God*, he admitted he had overvalued the bare necessities like food, water, clothing, and medicine.

> So many people . . . desperately needed more than the help that we were prepared to give. What they wanted even more . . . was for someone, anyone, even a stranger who was still trying to learn their language, to sit for a while, or just stand with them, and let them share their stories. I perhaps should have known this, but I was amazed to see the power of human presence. In my pride, I thought that I knew exactly what these people needed, but I never would have thought to put "conversation" or "human connection" on my list.[11]

Calvin Miller authored *The Valiant Papers*, an intriguing collection of observations by a guardian angel named Valiant. Focus: Earth. Valiant calls our planet "Muddyscuttle." His assignment is J. B., an unregenerate earthling.

Valiant cares about J. B. but yearns for heaven. Boasting masks his homesickness. Occasionally *and* ironically, he acknowledges an earthly treasure that we earthlings tend to discount.

> At . . . times J. B. would retreat to his room and cry.

> At such moments I hovered close to my small charge, finding my angelic nature a tremendous disadvantage. He needed the comfort of a flesh and blood physiology, and we guardians lack that blessed curse. . . . I craved at these moments the solid incarnation that our Logos once achieved. In human suffering there are times when materiality can serve best.

Angels cannot touch. Let the Committee remember this weakness. It is for this reason that the Logos became a man. . . . We cannot save what we cannot touch. It was skin that clothed the eternal nature and made our High Command touchable.[12]

Incarnation: The Ministry of Touch

Years ago, eternity past to be exact, God the Father foreknew what would beset mankind: sin. He knew how to solve our problem. His response was his Son; a "who," not a "what." John Oswalt noted, "[God] did not stand off and shout instructions. He came to us and bore our griefs and our sorrows."[13] Philip Yancey commented, "In Jesus, God gave us a face."[14]

After God's self-disclosure, a suffering Job worshiped again (42:1–6) for the first time since the first round of testing (1:20–21). Intimacy mattered more than his physical well-being or socio-economic status.

Thoughts to Ponder

"Now when Job's three friends heard of all this adversity that had come upon him, *they came* each one from his own place, Eliphaz the Temanite, Bildad the Shuhite and Zophar the Naamathite; and *they made an appointment together to come to sympathize with him and comfort him*. When they lifted up their eyes at a distance and did not recognize him, *they raised their voices and wept*. And each of them tore his robe and they threw dust over their heads toward the sky. Then *they sat down on the ground with him* for seven days and seven nights with *no one speaking a word to him*, for they saw that his pain was very great [italics mine]." (Job 2:11-13)

"Everyone must be quick to hear, slow to speak and slow to anger." (James 1:19)

2

Letting God Be God

I n his book *The Knowledge of the Holy*, A. W. Tozer tackled the doctrine of God. He divulged, "What comes into our minds when we think about God is the most important thing about us."[15] In the Prologue (Job 1–2), Satan challenged Job's "God picture." Accusation lurked behind the question, "Does Job fear God for nothing?" (1:9).

> *Satan*, a Hebrew noun, means "adversary." It appears twenty-seven times in the Old Testament, fourteen times in Job. Seven times *satan* refers to a human being (1 Samuel 29:4; 2 Samuel 19:22; 1 Kings 5:4; 11:14, 23, 25; Psalm 109:6).

Two rounds of testing would devastate Job, costing him everything dear. After each test, however, he honored God.

Round One – Job 1:21
Naked I came from my mother's womb, and naked I shall return there. The Lord gave and the Lord has taken away. Blessed be the name of the Lord.

Round Two – Job 2:10
Shall we indeed accept good from God and not accept adversity?

The narrator subsequently hailed Job.

Round One – Job 1:22
Through all this Job did not sin nor did he blame God.

Round Two – Job 2:10
In all this Job did not sin with his lips.

The adversary should have rephrased his question: "Do *Job's friends* fear God for nothing?" For one week, Eliphaz, Bildad, and Zophar had appeared "all ears." They were with Job, without talking (2:11–13). On the eighth day, Job spoke first, cursing his birthday (chap. 3), causing the friends to respond posthaste. All three presumed to be God's spokesman. No one waited for God to answer, i.e., to let God be God.

The title "Cycles of Dialogue," according to Old Testament scholars, refers to Job 4–27; a "Clash of Dogma," in my opinion: Job vs. Job's friends. This section of the book features sixteen speeches. The speeches of Eliphaz (3), Bildad (3), and Zophar (2) reveal glaring character flaws.

First, the friends preferred to sermonize, not sympathize. They *had been* quiet when Job sat, shocked and speechless, among the ashes. To be silent ≠ to listen. When Job eventually vented, Eliphaz, Bildad, and Zophar could not bite their tongues. They did not try.

Second, the friends glorified "orthodoxy" (lit., right belief). I interject, is orthodoxy the heartbeat of God? Eliphaz, Bildad, and Zophar would sing one theological tune, "The Doctrine of Divine Retribution" (description: two stanzas, no refrain, repeat *ad nauseam*).

Stanza #1 God blesses the righteous.
Stanza #2 God curses the wicked.

Mishandled by the friends, the doctrine of divine retribution wounded Job. Eliphaz, Bildad, and Zophar rationalized, "The truth, particularly Stanza #2, sometimes hurts. The sufferer must be a blasphemer!" Pronouncing Job guilty, the friends portrayed God as Supreme Vending Machine, the dispenser of Job's curses, because Job, by his conduct, had been inserting wicked "tokens." I interject, is not heaven's throne also the seat of mercy and the source of grace? In the Epilogue (42:7–17), God informed Eliphaz, "My anger burns against you and against your two friends, for you have not spoken of me what is right, as my servant Job has" (v. 7 ESV). One doctrine does not explain life. Two stanzas cannot summarize God.

Different Day, Same Problem

The writers Voltaire and Rudyard Kipling never met. Years and miles separated them. Nevertheless, they tackled the same absurdity. Voltaire chose prose: "If God made us in His image, we have certainly returned the compliment."[16] Kipling chose poetry:

In a land that the sand overlays—the ways to her gates are untrod—

A multitude ended their days whose fates were made splendid by God . . .

When the wine stirred in their heart their bosoms dilated,
They rose to suppose themselves kings over all things created—
To decree a new earth at a birth without labour or sorrow—
To declare: "We prepare it to-day and inherit to-morrow."
They chose themselves prophets and priests of minute under-
standing,
Men swift to see done, and outrun, their extremist command-
ing . . .

Swiftly these pulled down the walls that their fathers had made them—
The impregnable ramparts of old, they razed and relaid them . . .

They replied to their well-wishers' fears—to their enemies' laughter,
Saying: "Peace! We have fashioned a God Which shall save us hereafter."[17]

Voltaire and Kipling raise a legitimate issue, namely, what are divine caricatures?

Anthropomorphism

Throughout Scripture, especially the Old Testament, biblical characters and biblical writers expressed themselves anthropomorphically (italics are mine in the quotations below):

The Lord brought us out of Egypt with a mighty *hand* and an outstretched *arm* and with great terror and with signs and wonders. (Deuteronomy 26:8)

Then the channels of the sea appeared, the foundations of the world were laid bare, by the rebuke of the Lord, at the blast of the breath of His *nostrils*. (2 Samuel 22:16)

When I consider your heavens, the work of your *fingers*, the moon and the stars, which you have set in place. (Psalm 8:3 NIV)

The *eyes* of the Lord are toward the righteous and His *ears* are open to their cry. The *face* of the Lord is against evildoers, to cut off the memory of them from the earth. (Psalm 34:15–16)

In your love you kept me from the pit of destruction; you have put all my sins behind your *back*. (Isaiah 38:17 NIV)

This Jesus God raised up, and of that we all are witnesses. Being therefore exalted at the *right hand* of God, and having received from the Father the promise of the Holy Spirit, he has poured out this that you yourselves are seeing and hearing. (Acts 2:32–33 ESV)

And He put all things in subjection under [Christ's] *feet*, and gave Him as head over all things to the church, which is His body, the fullness of Him who fills all in all. (Ephesians 1:22–23)

Anthropomorphism is a type of personification.[18] It humanizes anything nonhuman. The prime example of a nonhuman is God.

Speaker: Prophet Balaam

God is not a man, that he should lie, or a son of man, that he should change his mind. Has he said, and will he not do it? Or has he spoken, and will he not fulfill it? (Numbers 23:19 ESV)

Speaker: Prophet Samuel
He who is the Glory of Israel does not lie or change his mind; for he is not a human being, that he should change his mind. (1 Samuel 15:29 NIV)

Speaker: God
"For My thoughts are not your thoughts, neither are your ways My ways," declares the Lord. "For as the heavens are higher than the earth, so are My ways higher than your ways, and My thoughts than your thoughts." (Isaiah 55:8–9)

Speaker: God
How can I give you up, O Ephraim? How can I surrender you, O Israel? How can I make you like Admah? How can I treat you like Zeboiim? My heart is turned over within Me, all my compassions are kindled. I will not execute My fierce anger; I will not destroy Ephraim again. For I am God and not man, the Holy One in your midst, and I will not come in wrath. (Hosea 11:8–9)

Speaker: Jesus
God is spirit, and his worshipers must worship in the Spirit and in truth. (John 4:24 NIV)

Writer: Apostle Paul
[Christ] is the image of the invisible God, the firstborn over all creation. (Colossians 1:15 NIV)

Throughout Scripture, especially the Old Testament, God described Himself anthropomorphically (italics are mine in the quotations below):

Then Moses said, "Now show me your glory." . . . "But," he said, "you cannot see my *face*, for no one may see me and live." Then the Lord said, "There is a place near me where you may stand on a rock. When my glory passes by, I will put you in a cleft in the rock and cover you with my *hand* until I have passed by. Then I will remove my *hand* and you will see my *back*; but my *face* must not be seen." (Exodus 33:18, 20–23 NIV)

The glory of Lebanon will come to you, the juniper, the box tree, and the cypress together, to beautify the place of My sanctuary; and I shall make the place of My *feet* glorious. (Isaiah 60:13)

Therefore, I indeed shall deal in wrath. My *eye* will have no pity nor shall I spare; and though they cry in My *ears* with a loud voice, yet I shall not listen to them. (Ezekiel 8:18)

He said: "Son of man, this is the place of my throne and the place for the *soles* of my *feet*. This is where I will live among the Israelites forever. The house of Israel will never again defile my holy name—neither they nor their kings—by their prostitution and the funeral offerings for their kings at their death." (Ezekiel 43:7 NIV)

Yet it is I who taught Ephraim to walk, I took them in My *arms*; but they did not know that I healed them. (Hosea 11:3)

These are the words of the Amen, the faithful and true witness, the ruler of God's creation. I know your deeds, that you are neither cold nor hot. I wish you were either one or the other! So, because you are lukewarm—neither hot nor cold—I am about to spit you out of my *mouth*. (Revelation 3:14–16 NIV)

Anthropomorphisms, therefore, do not offend God.

Idolatry

Idolatry, on the other hand, incites God's wrath. Remember the Ten Commandments? "You shall not make for yourself an idol, or any likeness of what is in heaven above or on the earth beneath or in the water under the earth. You shall not worship them or serve them; for I the Lord your God, am a jealous God" (Exodus 20:4–5).

In the land of Moab, the setting for Deuteronomy, Moses addressed the second generation of Israelites after the exodus from Egypt. He would soon pass away. They, led by Joshua, would soon cross over the Jordan River. Moses reminded them that the second commandment banned idolatrous depictions of the Lord God. "You saw no form of any kind the day the Lord spoke to you at Horeb out of the fire. Therefore watch yourselves very carefully, so that you do not become corrupt and make for yourselves an idol (Deuteronomy 4:15–16 NIV). An idol, lifeless and little, would misrepresent God, infinite and intimate.[19]An idol would mislead worshipers, insinuating that the sovereign God can be manipulated, even manhandled.[20]

Ever met a Christian that chiseled an idol? Neither have I. Do you know why? Manufacturing an idol would be a conspicuous sin: *easy* to recognize; therefore, *easier* to avoid.

Christian hands may be idle, but Christian minds have been busy: cozy with theology; carefree with convictions; concocting mental images rather than caricatures of wood, metal, stone, or clay. Hence, the apostle John rightly warned the church, "Guard yourselves from idols" (1 John 4:21).

The divine word at the beginning forbids that the Divine be likened to any of the things known by men,

since every concept which comes from some incomprehensible image by an approximate understanding and by
guessing at the divine nature constitutes an idol of God
and does not proclaim God.[21]

Personal Reasons

Distorted thoughts about God do harm. They not only dis-
honor Him but also inhibit us. In 1953, Anglican minister J. B.
Phillips authored *Your God Is Too Small*. Part One profiled twelve
destructive God pictures.

- Resident Policeman: deifying the nagging inner voice
  known as conscience
- Parental Hangover: fear of one's earthly father projected
  onto God
- Grand Old Man: old-fashioned or out of touch
- Meek and Mild: sentimental, never confrontational
- Absolute Perfection: perfectionist expecting perfection
- Heavenly Bosom: escape from reality
- God-in-a-Box: a good churchman (e.g., Baptist,
  Presbyterian, Lutheran)
- Managing Director: a magnified man too busy to focus
  on the details of anyone's life
- Secondhand God: accumulated ideas about God that do
  not derive from personal experiences with Him
- Perennial Grievance: one who always disappoints,
  therefore the one to blame
- Pale Galilean: one who takes all the joy out of living
- Projected Image: magnification of one's own good
  qualities

Phillips rightly reasoned, "If it is true that there is Someone
in charge of the whole mystery of life and death, we can hardly

expect to escape a sense of futility and frustration until we begin to see what He is like and what His purposes are."[22]

From Homeless Martyr to King

In his book *The Final Quest*, Rick Joyner recorded a series of God-given visions. Part V, titled "The Overcomers," is a dialogue between the author and the Lord in the great hall of judgment. The two walked while they talked. Various thrones lined their walkway. The Judgment Seat of Christ disappeared behind them.

When the Lord suddenly stopped, Joyner stopped, but his eyes roamed. Amazement! He recognized the occupant of a nearby throne, a man named Angelo. This "king" in heaven *had been* homeless on earth.

The Lord relished the opportunity to talk about Angelo. I understand why. Life or death or afterlife did not sway Angelo. The Lord stirred him.

> Angelo was a martyr every day that he lived. He would only do enough for himself to stay alive, and he gladly sacrificed his life to save a needy friend. . . . Angelo died every day because he did not live for himself, but for others. While on earth he always considered himself the least of the saints, but he was one of the greatest. . . . Angelo did not die for a doctrine, or even his testimony, but he did die for Me.[23]

What moves you?

Thoughts to Ponder

"I had heard of you by the hearing of the ear, but now my eye sees you." (Job 42:5 ESV)

"For now we see in a mirror dimly, but then face to face; now I know in part, but then I will know fully just as I also have been fully known." (1 Corinthians 13:12)

"For to me, to live is Christ, and to die is gain." (Philippians 1:21)

3

Keeping What Matters

On January 18, 1998, Dr. Don Musser warned the members of Central Baptist Church in Daytona Beach, Florida, "Trouble lurks when a good thing becomes an 'ism.'"[24] Consider two extremes: materialism and asceticism. Materialism values things more than anything else. Asceticism avoids things as moral contaminants, nothing else. Isn't there a middle ground? The book of Job provides invaluable insights, beginning with the fact that God gives us things.

Over a lifetime (1:3), Job amassed a fortune because God had blessed him (Job 1:9–10). Ascetics would expect Job to have been corrupted, to have become materialistic, but the books of Job and Ezekiel insist the rich man from Uz was "blameless" and "upright" (1:1, 8; 2:3) and righteous (Ezekiel 14:12–20).

In one afternoon, Job lost everything. Four of his servants were the bearer of bad news (Job 1:13–19). Materialists would expect Job to have lost the will to live, literally having nothing to live for, but the book of Job records how Job held his integrity tightly (2:3, 9; 27:2–6). Coordinated attacks on his character did not break him. The book of Job also records his passion for God. Like Jacob by the Jabbok River (Genesis 32:24–32), he contended with the Lord God. Like Moses at Mount Sinai (Exodus 33:18–23), he wanted a face-to-face meeting.

How does one explain Job's behavior?

The writer of Ecclesiastes, in chapter 3, listed fourteen pairings of events (vv. 1–8). Peter Seeger set them to music. The Byrds recorded Seeger's song "Turn! Turn! Turn!" in 1965. Twenty-four years later, John Grisham borrowed the phrase "a time to kill" for his first novel.

Each pair of times represents the rhythmic extremes of life. "A time to gain and a time to lose" could have been the fifteenth pairing. To live is to lose *sometimes*, but not every loss is bad. For a plant, losing blooms, leaves, or branches expedites new growth. For a snake, losing skin enables growth. Of course, people aren't plants or reptiles. Nevertheless, loss may not be a setback. Dieters celebrate weight loss. Without tooth loss, children would never get permanent teeth. Hair loss is not fatal; to this, I can testify.

Enterprise is a town in Southeast Alabama where the bizarre statue of a boll weevil greets drivers approaching the intersection of Main Street and College Street. Erected in 1919, it honors the pervasive pest that destroyed field after field of cotton, forcing the locals to diversify what they planted. Switching from cotton to peanuts, farmers soon reaped profits again. Substantial gains followed great losses.

Contrasting Responses to Possessions

The Diogenes Syndrome is spreading. You know it better as "hoarding." On April 6, 2016, police in Vigo, Spain, found the body of a fifty-one-year-old man crushed to death by twenty tons of falling stuff. The ceiling above his living room could no longer bear the weight. He died alone. Time of death: sadly unknown. A concerned Facebook friend contacted the local authorities from her home in the Canary Islands—thousands of miles away—when six days had passed without any online activity.[25]

My colleague Melinda Gann teaches mathematics. Don't let her petite physique fool you. She lives large. Recently, Melinda told my wife about winning a war against clutter, a more common menace. The decision to keep or to discard hinged upon her answering two questions:

- Is it useful?
- Does it bring me pleasure?

Watching Melinda work, her husband Don worried about his own future at their house.

Job's Response to Loss

Job suffered material loss (lots of livestock)—that which can be replaced—and personal loss (ten children)—that which cannot be replaced. Immediately afterwards, he worshiped, declaring, "The Lord has taken away" (Job 1:21). What Job said reflected his worldview: God is the cause, not God is culprit. When his health failed, Job reiterated that God is the cause while holding fast to his integrity (2:9–10). The Hebrew verb translated "hold fast" is a participle, denoting continuous action.

Job's wife acknowledged her husband's integrity. His friends did not, consequently inciting a war of words that raged from chapter 4 to chapter 27.

Speaker: Eliphaz

Is it because of your reverence that He reproves you, that He enters into judgment against you? Is not your wickedness great, and your iniquities without end? (22:4–5)

Speaker: Bildad

Lo, God will not reject a man of integrity, nor will He support the evildoers. (8:20)

Speaker: Zophar

Oh, how I wish that God would speak, that he would open his lips against you and disclose to you the secrets of wisdom, for true wisdom has two sides. Know this: God has even forgotten some of your sin. (11:5–6 NIV)

What would have happened if Eliphaz, Bildad, and Zophar had not "come to sympathize with [Job] and to comfort him" (2:11)? Sadly, we'll never know.

Job had good reason to clutch his integrity. "A good name is to be more desired than great riches" (Proverbs 22:1). "A good name is better than a good ointment" (Ecclesiastes 7:1).

Eventually, however, Job clutched his integrity too tightly. Theological crisis ensued. Carney and Long explained, "Job was not simply disoriented by the loss and wracked by pain. He felt that his most basic understanding of God and God's character was at stake. Certainly he could expect pain in this life, but *this much pain*? Certainly loss is a real part of human experience, but *such overwhelming loss?*"[26] Confident that he was innocent, Job concluded that God had mistreated him.

> Behold, I cry "Violence!" but I get no answer; I shout for help, but there is no justice. He has walled up my way so that I cannot pass; and He has put darkness on my paths. He has stripped my honor from me, and removed the crown from my head. He breaks me down on every side, and I am gone; and He has uprooted my hope like a tree. He has also kindled His anger against me, and considered me as His enemy. His troops come together, and build up their way against me, and camp around my tent. . . . My bone clings to my skin and my flesh, and I have escaped only by the skin of my teeth. Pity me, pity me, O you my friends, for the hand of God has struck me. Why do you persecute me as God does, and are not satisfied with my flesh? (Job 19:7–12, 20–22)

A seismological shift had occurred in Job's worldview: God became culprit.

Today, *that* conclusion leads people to walk away from the church. They turn into an apostate or an agnostic. Job never knew such options. To lose his relationship with God, even though God had angered him, was his worst-case scenario. Therefore, Job resolved, "Though [God] slay me, I will hope in him; yet I will argue my ways to his face." (13:15 ESV)

From the whirlwind, God finally spoke to Job, His first words since chapter 2, His first words to a human being in the story. God's silence had frustrated Job.

> If I called and God answered me, I cannot believe that he would give ear to my voice. (9:16)

> O that a hearing were given to me. Behold my mark— let the Almighty answer me. (31:35)

Without communication, a relationship cannot survive. Hence, when God spoke to Job, His speeches doubly assured Job that God, who is always close (i.e., omnipresent), still cared. His relationship with God had not ended; the reason that a diseased and destitute Job worshiped (42:1–6) well before God "returned" his fortunes (vv. 10–17), just before God vindicated him (vv. 7–9).

Job was a survivor. He countered his losses by pursuing that which lasts.

Discernment: The Appropriate Response to Gain and Loss

The standard of living in the United States is unprecedented: income, technology, opportunity, comforts, supply, options, and space. Even America's poor live better than most of the world. As a result, the "American dream" poses a daunting challenge: how does one handle affluence? Possessions can possess their owners.

- To whom much is given, much is required (Luke 12:48).
- To whom much has been given, loss will likely be more devastating.

Discernment can lessen the impact of loss; specifically, discerning between a need and a want, how the apostle Paul lived.

> Not that I speak from want; for I have learned to be content in whatever circumstances I am. I know how to get along with humble means, and I also know how to live in prosperity; in any and every circumstance I have learned the secret of being filled and going hungry, both of having abundance and suffering need. I can do all things through Him who strengthens me. And my God shall supply all your needs according to His riches in glory in Christ Jesus. (Philippians 4:10–13, 19)

Thoughts to Ponder

"For we have brought nothing into the world, so we cannot take anything out of it either." (1 Timothy 6:7)

"Indeed, I count everything as loss because of the surpassing worth of knowing Christ Jesus my Lord. For his sake I have suffered the loss of all things and count them as rubbish, in order that I may gain Christ." (Philippians 3:8 ESV)

"If the glories of Heaven were more real to us, if we lived less for material things and more for things eternal and spiritual, we would be less easily disturbed by this present life."[27] (Billy Graham)

4

Handling Chronic Pain:
When God Chooses *Not* to Heal

aul Brand and Philip Yancey coauthored three books. In
their third book, *Pain: The Gift Nobody Wants*, Brand, an
orthopedic surgeon, recalled a four-year-old patient named
Tanya. She had dark eyes, curly hair, and an impish smile. Her
swollen left ankle rotated freely, fully dislocated, but she never
flinched. Ulcers covered the soles of her feet—infected, oozing,
bone exposed—but she never winced. Tanya had been born with
a rare genetic defect: "congenital indifference to pain." Before adolescence, she would be institutionalized. Legs amputated. Hands
blistered. Fingers missing. Elbows dislocated. Tongue lacerated
and scarred. Dr. Brand understandably asserted, "I . . . regard pain
as one of the most remarkable design features of the human body.
. . . I do not desire, and cannot even imagine, a life without pain.
. . . Thank God for pain."[28]

When pain alerts us that we aren't well or warns us of severe
injury, it is a blessing. Anything chronic, however, can be a curse.

Second Round of Testing: Chronic Disease

After the first round of testing, Job mourned and worshiped. He didn't sin (Job 1:22); the adversary had alleged he would curse God *to his face* (v. 11).

Job's righteous reaction to staggering suffering prompted God to scold the adversary. "He still holds fast his integrity, although you incited Me against him, to ruin him without cause" (2:3).

Unfazed and unimpressed, the adversary complained that Job had not suffered enough. He proposed a better test: "Stretch out your hand and touch his bone and his flesh, and he will curse you to your face" (v. 5 ESV). God surprisingly consented.

Diagnosing what ailed Job is difficult because the scripture provides few facts. According to the text, it was dermatological. The Hebrew noun, typically translated "boil" or "sore," occurs thirteen times in the Old Testament, affecting humans (Leviticus 13:18–20, 23; Deuteronomy 28:27, 35; 2 Kings 20:7; Job 2:7; Isaiah 38:21) as well as animals (Exodus 9:9–11).[29] Hezekiah's condition was terminal (2 Kings 20:1–7; Isaiah 38:1–22); Job's was not because God had ordered the adversary, "Spare his life" (Job 2:6).

Job recounted his symptoms twice.

My flesh is clothed with worms and a crust of dirt; my skin hardens and runs. (7:5)

At night it pierces my bones within me, and my gnawing pains take no rest. . . . My skin turns black on me, and my bones burn with fever. (30:17, 30)

Watts, Owens, and Tate pointed out, "Ancient peoples had no knowledge of modern medical diagnoses. These terms for diseases were general ones which described rather than diagnosed."[30] Habel added, "Job's own language about his bodily and psychological afflictions is not medical but poetic."[31] He even theorized that the sickness had no earthly parallel because the adversary caused it.[32]

"Did God heal Job?" is a bigger mystery than "what did Job have?" The Epilogue records Job's restoration (42:10–17), but it never mentions his health.

Terminal vs. Chronic: Physical and Psychological Ramifications

An obvious difference between a terminal illness and a chronic one is quantity of life. At the same time, a significant similarity is quality of life; namely, the lack of it. Both the dying patient and the daily struggler suffer, but the daily struggler suffers longer.

Chronic illness may not kill, but it can steal one's joy and ultimately one's will to live. I saw firsthand how lower back pain, lupus, and rheumatoid arthritis hampered my mother. She didn't complain, but every day was difficult as she dealt with unrelenting stiffness and pain. What tormented my mother didn't take her life. A stroke did.

Chronic illness may also affect one's mind. On its website, the American Psychological Association acknowledges that chronic pain, for instance, can cause feelings like anger, sadness, hopelessness, and anxiety.[33] Such feelings now characterize Somatic Symptom Disorder.[34] Dr. Robert Benninger commented, "It is common to find in seriously ill patients certain mental changes brought on through prolonged suffering. This could have been so in Job's affliction."[35]

Chronic: Spiritual Implications

God heals because He can and because He cares. A chronic illness, therefore, can become a theological dilemma: God has chosen not to heal. To ask why often leads daily strugglers to unhealthy conclusions.

1. **God is punishing me.**
    Consequences: Guilt and Fear
2. **God has ignored my prayers.**
    Consequence: Anger
3. **God no longer values me.**
    Consequence: Despair

Paul encountered God's decision not to heal. In 2 Corinthians, he cryptically referred to a "thorn in the flesh," the result of a satanic attack. Though the apostle had prayed without ceasing, God denied his request, assuring him, "My grace is sufficient for you, for my power is made perfect in weakness" (12:9 ESV).

What is striking is that which happened next. Paul worshiped God.

> Therefore, I will boast all the more gladly of my weaknesses, so that the power of Christ may rest upon me. For the sake of Christ, then, I am content with weaknesses, insults, hardships, persecutions, and calamities. For when I am weak, then I am strong. (vv. 9–10 ESV)

God used Paul's righteous reaction to convict me. Facing my own aches and pains (nothing life-threatening) from time to time, I have prayed for healing, as the apostle did—according to verse 8—three times. Yet, unlike the apostle, I had not worshiped while I hurt. I had been stuck at verse 8, failing to move past verse 8 to verses 9–10.

Because God convicted me, I resolved to modify how I prayed. Two additional requests now accompany my prayers for healing without exception: *God, grow me during trials,* and *God, glorify yourself through afflictions.*

Dan Hall is the pastor of Livingston Fellowship in Flora, Mississippi, and an executive coach. He hails from Texas but lives in Mississippi. On August 16, 2015, a pulmonary embolism caused him to pass out at a hotel in Houston. The subsequent fall while unconscious injured his spinal cord.

Dan's new normal could not be any more different. He once stood 6'4". He now sits, a paraplegic strapped to a wheelchair. Interviewed for *Mississippi Christian Living* magazine, Dan smiled as he testified, "There are moments that I get really overwhelmed that God can trust me with this [disability]. As I look ahead I struggle emotionally, but I don't feel depressed."[36]

Thoughts to Ponder

"O Nebuchadnezzar, we do not need to give you an answer concerning this matter. If it be so, our God whom we serve is able to deliver us from the furnace of blazing fire; and He will deliver us out of your hand, O king. But even if He does not, let it be known to you, O king, that we are not going to serve your gods or worship the golden image that you have set up." (Daniel 3:16-18)

"Though the fig tree should not blossom, and there be no fruit on the vines, though the yield of the olive should fail, and the fields produce no food, though the flock should be cut off from the fold, and there be no cattle in the stalls, yet I will exult in the Lord. I will rejoice in the God of my salvation. The Lord God is my strength, and He has made my feet like hinds' feet, and makes me walk on my high places." (Habakkuk 3:17-19)

"My Father, if it be possible, let this cup pass from me; nevertheless, not as I will, but as you will." (Matthew 26:39 ESV)

5

Time-Out:
Addressing the Elephant in the Room

"Why do the wicked prosper?" and "Why do bad things happen to good people?" are not new questions. The Old Testament wrestled with the problem of evil. Listen to the psalmist:

Surely God is good to Israel, to those who are pure in heart! But as for me, my feet came close to stumbling; my steps had almost slipped. For I was envious of the arrogant, as I saw the prosperity of the wicked. For there are no pains in their death; and their body is fat. They are not in trouble as other men; nor are they plagued like mankind. Therefore pride is their necklace; the garment of violence covers them. Their eye bulges from fatness; the imaginations of their heart run riot. They mock, and wickedly speak of oppression; they speak from on high. They have set their mouth against the heavens, and their tongue parades through the earth. (73:1–9)

Listen to Ecclesiastes:

There is something else meaningless that occurs on earth: the righteous who get what the wicked deserve, and the wicked who get what the righteous deserve. This too, I say, is meaningless. (8:14 NIV)

Listen to Habakkuk:

O Lord, how long shall I cry for help, and you will not hear? Or cry to you "Violence!" and you will not save? Why do you make me see iniquity, and why do you idly look at wrong? Destruction and violence are before me; strife and contention arise. So the law is paralyzed, and justice never goes forth. For the wicked surround the righteous; so justice goes forth perverted. (1:2–4 ESV)

When Adam and Eve fell, the curse of sin pervaded creation. Death entered the world (Romans 5:12–21) and all manner of suffering accompanied it.

Since Adam and Eve, "There is none righteous, not even one" (3:10). Paul, writing to the church at Rome, didn't quote Psalm 14 or 53 to solve the problem of evil. Nevertheless, some Christians cite the apostle or Jesus (see Luke 18:18–19), insisting that bad things do not happen to good people because "No one is good." Case closed!

The problem of evil isn't that simple. As proof, brilliant minds—unbelievers and believers, liberal or conservative—have tried to solve it but did not.

1. Irenaeus, *Against Heresies*
2. Augustine, *The City of God*
3. Thomas Aquinas, *Summa Theologica*

4. Friedrich Schleiermacher, *The Christian Faith*
5. Gottfried Leibniz, *Theodicy: Essays on the Goodness of God, the Freedom of Man and the Origin of Evil*
6. C. S. Lewis, *The Problem of Pain*
7. John Hick, *Evil and the Love of God*
8. Harold S. Kushner, *When Bad Things Happen to Good People*
9. Alvin Plantinga, God, *Freedom, and Evil*
10. James Dobson, *When God Doesn't Make Sense*
11. Norman L. Geisler, *If God, Why Evil?: A New Way to Think about the Question*
12. James L. Crenshaw, *Defending God*
13. N. T. Wright, *Evil and the Justice of God*
14. William Hasker, *The Triumph of God Over Evil*

This excursus does not offer yet another solution to the problem of evil. It isn't a theodicy; i.e., a defense of God as good despite the existence of evil. Its purpose is to provide context for the book of Job.

What Is the Problem of Evil?

Human beings experience two kinds of suffering: (1) consequences of one's behavior and (2) circumstances beyond one's control.

As sinners, we reap what we sow (Galatians 6:7), regrettable yet deserved. Whatever the adversity might be, the Bible identifies it as judgment, not coincidence. Deuteronomy 28:22–24, for example, forewarned the Israelites:

The Lord will smite you with consumption and with fever and with inflammation and with fiery heat and with the sword and with blight and with mildew, and they shall pursue you until you perish. And the heaven which is over your head shall be bronze, and the earth which is under you, iron. The Lord will make the rain of your land powder and dust; from heaven it shall come down on you until you are destroyed.

The ones being judged, however, were usually oblivious or in denial.

Ephraim mixes himself with the nations; Ephraim has become a cake not turned. Strangers devour his strength, yet he does not know it; grey hairs also are sprinkled on him, yet he does not know it. (Hosea 7:8–9)

You have sown much, but harvest little; you eat, but there is not enough to be satisfied; you drink, but there is not enough to become drunk; you put on clothing, but no one is warm enough; and he who earns, earns wages to put into a purse with holes. Thus says the Lord of hosts, "Consider your ways!" (Haggai 1:6–7)

Eliphaz, Bildad, and Zophar assumed that God was punishing Job; a reason they became upset at Job. How could he be unaware?

Speaker: Eliphaz

Your words have helped the tottering to stand, and you have strengthened feeble knees. But now it has come to you, and you are impatient; it touches you, and you are dismayed. Behold, how happy is the man whom God reproves, so do not despise the discipline of the Almighty. (Job 4:4–5; 5:17)

Speaker: Bildad

How long will you hunt for words? Show understanding and then we can talk. (18:2)

Speaker: Zophar

Are all these words to go unanswered? Is this talker to be vindicated? Will your idle talk reduce others to silence? Will no one rebuke you when you mock? You say to God, "My beliefs are flawless and I am pure in your sight." (11:2–4 NIV)

That the friends, rather than Job, were oblivious is a textbook example of irony. We the readers know more than any human character in the story. We owe our awareness to the narrator; after each round of testing, he inserted a declaration of Job's innocence.

Round One – Job 1:22
Through all this Job did not sin nor did he blame God.

Round Two – Job 2:10
In all this Job did not sin with his lips.

Eliphaz, Bildad, and Zophar focused on Job's sinfulness to prove their point that God punishes the wicked. They were right that their friend was a sinner but wrong that a specific sin or sins had caused his suffering.

Adam's sin had spread to Job's generation. It has reached ours, too. Consequently, everyone since Genesis 3 has lived in a fallen world. "Fallen" means the forces of nature pose an indiscriminate threat to all life on earth (Genesis 3:17–19; Romans 8:18–22). During the first round of testing, the "fire of God" (i.e., lightning) torched Job's sheep and a wilderness wind toppled the house where his children had gathered. "Fallen" also means that any sinner's sin can affect us. During the first round of testing, the Sabeans and the Chaldeans stole from Job.

An additional undeserved, adverse circumstance receives attention in the New Testament: Christians may endure persecution because they are Christians.

> Blessed are those who have been persecuted for the sake of righteousness, for theirs is the kingdom of heaven. Blessed are you when men cast insults at you, and persecute you, and say all kinds of evil against you falsely, on account of Me. Rejoice, and be glad, for your reward in heaven is great, for so they persecuted the prophets who were before you. (Matthew 5:10–12)

Jesus apprised the Twelve, "If you were of the world, the world would love you as its own; but because you are not of the world, but I chose you out of the world, therefore the world hates you" (John 15:19 ESV).

Years later, intense religious intolerance prompted Peter to write 1 Peter. He counseled the churches of northern Asia Minor (modern-day Turkey), "Keep your conduct among the Gentiles honorable, so that when they speak against you as evildoers, they may see your good deeds and glorify God on the day of visitation" (2:12 ESV).

Biblical Responses to the Problem of Evil

The problem of evil is a conundrum that intrigues intellectuals. Hence, a host of theological and philosophical positions exist now, but biblical responses matter more to Christians. The book of Job gives four of the six biblical answers to the quandary of suffering.

Testing of One's Faith

If Job hadn't been righteous, the two rounds of tragedy would not have occurred. The adversary did not doubt *that* Job feared

God; he questioned *why* Job feared. God, therefore, allowed the adversary to harm a faithful follower, the purpose being to reveal Job's motives.

In Genesis 22, God had subjected Abraham to a horrific test. According to James, testing should be a reason to rejoice (James 1:2–4). Abraham did regard his test as an opportunity to worship (Genesis 22:5). Job did, too.

Consequences of Sinfulness

Eliphaz, Bildad, and Zophar wrongly accused Job, but they were right that God punishes sin. The fate of the wicked was their favorite subject, based upon what preoccupied them when they spoke to Job.

	GOD	JOB	WICKED
ELIPHAZ			
1st Cycle	4:9, 17–18; 5:8–20	4:2–7; 5:1, 19–27	4:8–11, 17–21; 5:2–7, 12–16
2nd Cycle	15:4b, 8a, 11a, 13, 15, 25–26	15:2–13	15:14–16, 20–35
3rd Cycle	22:2–4, 12, 18a, 21–27	22:3–11, 13–15, 21–30	22:15–20
TOTAL	**33 Verses**	**50 Verses**	**45 Verses**
BILDAD			
1st Cycle	8:3–6, 13a, 20–21	8:2, 5–10, 21–22	8:11–19, 20b, 22
2nd Cycle	18:21b	18:2–4	18:5–21
3rd Cycle	25:2–6	no mention	no mention
TOTAL	**12 Verses**	**12 Verses**	**27.5 Verses**
ZOPHAR			
1st Cycle	11:5–11, 13	11:2–7, 13–19	11:11, 20
2nd Cycle	20:15, 23, 28–29	20:3–4	20:5–29
TOTAL	**12 Verses**	**15 Verses**	**27 Verses**

Focus of Job's Friends

Sanctification

During the Cycles of Dialogue, Job's hope waned (see Table below). His seventh speech recorded in chapters 23–24 was the final time he, being hopeful, believed he would be vindicated. Job

23:10 concludes, "When [God] has tried me, I shall come forth as gold." Peter and James, in like manner, encouraged persecuted Christians.

> You have been distressed by various trials, that the proof of your faith, being more precious than gold which is perishable, even though tested by fire, may be found to result in praise and glory and honor at the revelation of Jesus Christ. (1 Peter 1:6–7)

> Consider it all joy, my brethren, when you encounter various trials, knowing that the testing of your faith produces endurance. And let endurance have its perfect result, that you may be perfect and complete, lacking in nothing. (James 1:2–4)

Jesus himself "learned obedience from the things which He suffered" (Hebrews 5:8).

Author and apologist Nabeel Qureshi exhibited the same mindset as Job, posting the following message on Facebook:

> This is an announcement that I never expected to make, but God in His infinite and sovereign wisdom has chosen me for *this refining* [italics mine], and I pray He will be glorified through my body and my spirit. My family and I have received the news that I have advanced stomach cancer, and the clinical prognosis is quite grim.[37]

Qureshi passed away thirteen months later.

	GRIEF	AVOWAL OF INNOCENCE	HOPEFULNESS
FIRST CYCLE			
1st Speech	6:2–3, 8–9, 11–13, 7:1–6, 11	6:10, 24–26, 28–30; 7:20a	no mention
2nd Speech	9:25–27; 10:1, 15b, 17b–22	9:20–21; 10:7	no mention
3rd Speech	14:1–2, 7–12	12:4; 13:16, 18	13:13–15, 17, 19; 14:13–17
Total	**32 verses**	**13.5 verses**	**10 verses**
SECOND CYCLE			
4th Speech	16:6, 8b, 15–17, 20, 22; 17:1–2, 7–8, 11–16	16:15–17	16:18–19, 21; 17:9
5th Speech	19:14–20	no mention	19:25–29
6th Speech	21:6–17a, 18, 23–26, 30–33	no mention	no mention
Total	**44 verses**	**3 verses**	**9 verses**
THIRD CYCLE			
7th Speech	24:2–12a, 13–20	23:10–12	23:3–7, 17
8th Speech	no mention	27:2–6	no mention
Total	**19.5 verses**	**8 verses**	**6 verses**

Content of Job's Speeches in the Cycles of Dialogue

Getting One's Attention

C. S. Lewis emphasized, "God whispers to us in our pleasures, speaks in our conscience, but shouts in our pains: it is His megaphone to rouse a deaf world."[38] Elihu, a later character in the story, had conveyed the same message to Job.

Why do you complain against Him, that He does not give an account of all His doings? Indeed God speaks once, or twice, yet no one notices it. In a dream, a vision of the night, when sound sleep falls on men, while they slumber in their beds, then He opens the ears of men, and seals their instruction, that He may turn man aside from his conduct, and keep man from pride; He keeps back his soul from the pit, and his life from passing over into Sheol. Man is also chastened with pain on his bed, and with unceasing complaint in his bones; so that his life loathes bread, and his soul favorite food. His flesh wastes away from sight, and his bones which were not seen stick out. Then his soul draws near to the pit, and his life to those who bring death. . . . Behold, God does all these oftentimes with men, to bring back his soul from the pit, that he may be enlightened with the light of life. (Job 33:13–22, 29–30)

Glorifying God

Deuteronomic Theology, based upon Deuteronomy 27–28, popularized the causal link between behavior and consequences. Its proponents and opponents eventually clashed; Israel's Wisdom Movement would be the forum.

Proverbs espouses Deuteronomic Theology. Proverbs 12:21, for instance, contends, "No harm befalls the righteous, but the wicked are filled with trouble."

Job and Ecclesiastes dissent loudly. Ecclesiastes 7:15, for instance, laments, "I have seen everything during my lifetime of futility; there is a righteous man who perishes in his righteousness, and there is a wicked man who prolongs his life in his wickedness."[39] In the book of Job, Job (opponent) and his friends (proponents) personified the debate.

More than Job or Ecclesiastes, Jesus discouraged jumping to a Deuteronomic conclusion. In John 9, He and His disciples encountered a blind man. The disciples asked, "Rabbi, who *sinned* [italics mine], this man or his parents, that he should be born blind?" (v. 2). Jesus said, "It was neither that this man sinned, nor his parents; but it was in order that the works of God might be displayed in him" (v. 3; see also 11:1–4). Displaying God's power inspired Paul to bear his thorn in the flesh (2 Corinthians 12:1–10).

Consequences of Living in a Fallen World

On another occasion that only appears in Luke's Gospel, Jesus discouraged jumping to a Deuteronomic conclusion. The thirteenth chapter opens with an example of tyranny: Pontius Pilate had slaughtered an undisclosed number of Galileans. Jesus, a Galilean, did not criticize the Roman prefect but used the current event as a teachable moment.

> Do you suppose that these Galileans were greater sinners than all other Galileans, because they suffered this fate? I tell you, no, but, unless you repent, you will all likewise perish. Or do you suppose that those eighteen on whom the tower in Siloam fell and killed them, were worse culprits than all the men who live in Jerusalem? I tell you, no, but, unless you repent, you will all likewise perish. (Luke 13:2–5)

Why the Answers Are Not Enough

Christians, despite having the *right* answers, struggle much with the problem of evil. The obvious reason is that no one, faithful or infidel, likes to hurt. What can compare to trouble free?

Another reason is that every answer is overrated. "Inquiring minds want to know," but knowing why neither changes the past (what might have been) nor the present (how much pain one actually feels). Therefore, Humphreys reasoned,

> I confess that when I suffer I am not very concerned about why suffering has come to me. I am not concerned about an explanation. A blind man does not want explanations; he wants to see. It is not the origin of suffering that concerns us, but its destiny. We need to know where it is going more than where it has come from. Will it finally be destroyed, or is suffering the final reality?[40]

Explaining evil usually sounds like explaining it away, and Christians must never do that. Evil needs to be destroyed, not discussed. We believe that God has destroyed evil.[41]

What makes a trying situation tougher is not knowing which of the biblical answers applies when it matters most: in the throes of agony. Job's reality was worse; he never knew why. As time passes, perspective does improve, but hindsight isn't always 20/20.

To suffer is the human condition. Nevertheless, there is no such thing as a fair share of pain. God lets some folk suffer more than others. He intervenes with a miracle to prevent a tragedy *sometimes*. He heals to end an ordeal *sometimes*. Consequently, the "child" in us all instinctively protests, "Not fair!"

Peter protested. In John 21, the resurrected Jesus had told him how he would die: "Truly, truly, I say to you, when you were younger, you used to gird yourself, and walk wherever you wished; but when you grow old, you will stretch out your hands, and someone else will gird you, and bring you where you do not wish to go" (v. 18). Peter, seeing John, asked, "Lord, and what about this man?" (v. 21). Jesus answered, "If I want him to remain until I come, what is that to you? You follow me!" (v. 22).

Before Jesus, no one suffered as much as Job did. What answer would have been satisfactory to the diseased, destitute dad grieving the death of his children? By communicating with Job, God satisfied him.

6

Knowing How to Minister

In 1996, Robert J. Morgan authored the study *Empowered Parenting: Raising Kids in the Nurture and Instruction of the Lord.* He titled chapter twelve "Painful Parenting: When Your Children Break Your Heart." "When" rather than "if" became real for Robert and his wife Katrina. One of their three daughters struggled somewhat spiritually while away at college. Morgan turned his heartbreak into help, writing the book *Prayers and Promises for Worried Parents: Hope for Your Prodigal, Help for You* in 2003.

Regarding suffering, "when" rather than "if" pertains to all people. Tragedy, as a result, unites us and divides us. Of course, it unites us because heartbreak doesn't discriminate. We all have a "story." It also divides us into two categories whenever someone's everything falls apart: sufferers and comforters.

Job's Friends: Starting Well and Finishing Poorly

"With friends like these, who needs enemies?" The criticism of Eliphaz, Bildad, and Zophar understandably has been harsh. Critics, however, fail to see how well they did *initially*.

- Job's friends left their families and their livelihood.
- Job's friends risked their lives, traveling to Uz at their own expense.
- Job's friends sacrificed a lot of time for Job.
- Job's friends sat silently with Job for seven days and seven nights.

According to verse 11 in chapter 2, Eliphaz, Bildad, and Zophar had intended "to sympathize . . . and comfort" their friend. The Hebrew verb *nud*, translated as "sympathize," depicts a back and forth movement, aptly describing a sympathizer shaking his head compassionately or grieving with a quivering lip (Job 16:5).[42] The Hebrew verb *nacham*, translated as "comfort," originally indicated "breathing deeply . . . the physical display of one's feelings."[43] Both verbs also appear together in 42:11.

The friends soon failed to do what they had intended to do. The Cycles of Dialogue reveal why. They, during their silence, had judged Job. They then waited for a confession of sins.

Meanwhile, Job misjudged his friends. He assumed that they could listen because they hadn't talked. Talkers are not good listeners, but listening is more than simply not talking.

When Job cursed the day of his birth (3:1), the friends were flabbergasted, shocked by what Job said and exasperated by what he did not say. Censuring and silencing Job replaced sympathizing and comforting him.

Attention Comforters: Silence Is Golden

After interviewing terminal patients for years, Elisabeth Kubler-Ross published her observations in the book titled *On Death and Dying* (1969). She proposed that a dying person passes through five "stages of grief": denial, anger, bargaining, depression, and acceptance. In the Prologue, following each round of testing, Job's behavior compares to denial. Beginning with the First Monologue (Job 3), he sounds angry.

Let the day perish on which I was to be born, and the night which said, "A boy is conceived." May that day be darkness; let not God above care for it, nor light shine on it. Let darkness and black gloom claim it; let a cloud settle on it; let the blackness of the day terrify it. As for that night let darkness seize it; let it not rejoice among the days of the year; let it not come into the number of the months. Behold, let that night be barren; let no joyful shout enter it. Let those curse it who curse the day, who are prepared to rouse Leviathan. Let the stars of its twilight be darkened; let it wait for light but have none, neither let it see the breaking dawn; because it did not shut the opening of my mother's womb, or hide trouble from my eyes. . . .

Why is light given to him who suffers, and life to the bitter of soul; who long for death, but there is none, and dig for it more than for hidden treasures; who rejoice greatly, they exult when they find the grave? Why is light given to a man whose way is hidden, and whom God has hedged in? For my groaning comes at the sight of my food, and my cries pour out like water. For what I fear comes upon me, and what I dread befalls me. I am not at ease, nor am I quiet, and I am not at rest, but turmoil comes. (vv. 3–10, 20–26)

How logical is a sufferer whose grief is fresh? One ought to ask, "Is Job lucid?" Eliphaz, Bildad, and Zophar never did. They absurdly jumped to conclusions though *their* circumstances permitted a reasoned assessment of the situation.

The friends somehow "heard" (2:11) about Job's misfortune. Like them, we all will get that emergency call. One need not be a member of the clergy. Unlike them, we should heed Proverbs 10:19: "He who restrains his lips is wise."

Resist the urge to offer "bumper sticker" theology.

- "Everything happens for a reason."
- "You have to look through the rain to see the rainbow."
- "When the going gets tough, the tough get going."
- "If life gives you lemons, make lemonade."

Handle Scripture with care. For the sake of illustration, read the following passage from Deuteronomy.

> Your ox shall be slaughtered before your eyes, but you shall not eat of it; your donkey shall be torn away from you, and shall not be restored to you; your sheep shall be given to your enemies, and you shall have none to save you. Your sons and your daughters shall be given to another people, while your eyes shall look on and yearn for them continually; but there shall be nothing you can do. A people whom you do not know shall eat up the produce of your ground and all your labors, and you shall never be anything but oppressed and crushed continually. And you shall be driven mad by the sight of what you see. The Lord will strike you on the knees and legs with sore boils, from which you cannot be healed, from the sole of your foot to the crown of your head. (28:31–35)

It sounds like a play-by-play of Job's ordeal. Applying it to his life, however, would be incorrect: to reckon that God has cursed Job for being wicked.

Final Instructions

Every quarter, Baylor University, my alma mater, mails me *Baylor Magazine*. Each issue concludes with "Alumni News & Updates," which includes obituaries. I have read them all, every word, though I don't know most of the deceased. My habit probably seems odd, even morbid. What strikes me is that the notices, now online, commonly mention a tragedy or two: e.g., "_____ [insert name] was preceded in death by her husband _____ [insert name] and her son _____ [insert name]."

To live like Job, "full of days" (42:17), means plenty of opportunities to play the roles of sufferer and comforter. If you're the sufferer, don't worry about what you say. If you're the comforter, be careful what you say.

Thoughts to Ponder

"You are worthless physicians, all of you! If only you would be altogether silent! For you, that would be wisdom." (Job 13:4-5 NIV)

"It is hard to know what to say to a person who has been struck by tragedy, but it is easier to know what not to say."[44] (Harold S. Kushner)

"Oh, the comfort–the inexpressible comfort of feeling *safe* with a person–having neither to weigh thoughts nor measure words, but pouring them all right out, just as they are, chaff and grain together; certain that a faithful hand will take and sift them, keep what is worth keeping, and then with the breath of kindness blow the rest away."[45] (Dinah Maria Craik)

"I love the Lord, because He hears my voice and my supplications. Because He has inclined His ear to me, therefore I shall call upon Him as long as I live." (Psalm 116:1-2)

7

Being Honest with God

In 1978, singer-songwriter Billy Joel released *52nd Street*, his sixth studio album and first No. #1 record. Three of its songs became Top 40 hits. "Honesty," a piano ballad, is the second track. Its heartfelt lyrics lament the scarcity of honesty.[46]

The question "Why is dishonesty prevalent?" has many answers; some of them, believe it or not, are noble. Telling the truth can be hurtful. Consequently, being *less* opinionated may be prudent when asked "Did you like the meatloaf?" or "Should I lose five pounds?" or "Do I look younger in this dress?" Telling the truth can be disrespectful. Thus, talking back to one's parents or giving the boss a piece of one's mind will not be profitable.

In the 1992 film *A Few Good Men*, Jack Nicholson's character bellows, "You can't handle the truth!" That famous line may be true about humans, but it isn't true about God. Job discovered this firsthand.

"Did You Hear What Job Said about God?"

After each round of testing, Job's respect for God's sovereignty did not waver. He even worshiped God *as* he mourned the death of his children. How he behaved warranted what the narrator and God had attested: "That man was blameless, upright, fearing God, and turning away from evil" (Job 1:1, 8; 2:3).

Beginning with the First Monologue, Job's attitude changed drastically. Criticism of God supplanted his esteem for God.

> When I think my bed will comfort me and my couch will ease my complaint, even then you frighten me with dreams and terrify me with visions, so that I prefer strangling and death, rather than this body of mine. (7:13–15 NIV)

> What is man, that you make so much of him, and that you set your heart on him, visit him every morning and test him every moment? How long will you not look away from me, nor leave me alone till I swallow my spit? If I sin, what do I do to you, you watcher of mankind? Why have you made me your mark? Why have I become a burden to you? (vv. 17–20 ESV)

> For He bruises me with a tempest, and multiplies my wounds without cause. He will not allow me to get my breath, but saturates me with bitterness. (9:17–18)

> It is all one; therefore I say, "He destroys the guiltless and the wicked." If the scourge kills suddenly, He mocks the despair of the innocent. The earth is given into the hand of the wicked; He covers the faces of its judges, if it is not He, then who is it? (vv. 22–24)

> As water wears away stones and torrents wash away the soil, so you destroy a person's hope. You overpower them once for all, and they are gone; you change their counte-

nance and send them away. If their children are honored, they do not know it; if their offspring are brought low, they do not see it. They feel but the pain of their own bodies and mourn only for themselves. (14:19–22 NIV)

I was at ease, but He shattered me, and He has grasped me by the neck and shaken me to pieces; He has also set me up as His target. His arrows surround me. Without mercy He splits my kidneys open; He pours out my gall on the ground. He breaks through me with breach after breach; He runs at me like a warrior. I have sewed sackcloth over my skin, and thrust my horn in the dust. My face is flushed with weeping, and deep darkness is on my eyelids, although there is no violence in my hands, and my prayer is pure. (16:12–17)

Know then that God has wronged me, and has closed His net around me. Behold, I cry, "Violence!" but I get no answer; I shout for help, but there is no justice. He has walled up my way so that I cannot pass; and He has put darkness on my paths. He has stripped my honor from me, and removed the crown from my head. He breaks me down on every side, and I am gone; and He has uprooted my hope like a tree. He has also kindled His anger against me, and considered me as His enemy. His troops come together, and build up their way against me, and camp around my tent. (19:6–12)

My skin and my flesh cling to my bones; I have escaped by the skin of my teeth. Have mercy on me, my friends, have mercy, for God's hand has struck me. Why do you persecute me as God does? Will you never get enough of my flesh? (vv. 20–22 HCSB)

From the city men groan, and the souls of the wounded cry out; yet God does not pay attention to folly. (24:12)

He wrongs the barren woman, and does no good for the widow. But He drags off the valiant by His power; He rises, but no one has assurance of life. (vv. 21–22)

The contrast between what Job said before and after chapter 3 has been too hard for some scholars to reconcile. As a result, they question the book's literary integrity. Harold Louis Ginsberg, for example, referred to Books of Job: Book of Job the Patient (JP) and Book of Job the Impatient (JIP).[47] Marvin Pope opined,

> The Prologue presents to us the traditional pious and patient saint who retained his composure and maintained his integrity through all the woes inflicted on him and refused to make any accusation of injustice against Yahweh, but rather continued to bless the god [sic] who had afflicted him. In the Dialogue we meet quite a different Job whose bitter complaints and charges of injustice against God shock his pious friends who doggedly defend divine justice and persistently reaffirm the doctrine of exact individual retribution. In view of these attitudes, the Epilogue, in which the friends, not Job, are rebuked for not having spoken the truth about Yahweh comes as something of a shock.[48]

"Did You Hear What Other Old Testament Saints Said about God?"

William of Occam maintained, "*Pluralitas non est ponenda sine necessitate*," translated as "Plurality should not be posited without necessity." Occam's "Razor" promotes simplicity.[49] The simplest answer (most obvious) is often the best answer.

1. **The desktop computer doesn't work.**
   Complex: The CPU has died.
   Simple: Is it plugged in? Has the breaker been tripped?

2. **My son is failing this semester.**
   Complex: All of his professors have conspired against him.
   Simple: Has he gone to class? Is he studying?

3. **My car quit.**
   Complex: I think I need a new alternator.
   Simple: Check the fuel gauge.

4. **I have a recurring headache.**
   Complex: I may have an aneurysm.
   Simple: What's your stress level?

Regarding the change in Job's demeanor, to theorize that different authors are responsible for conflicting books about Job that, somehow merging, formed the book of Job more qualifies as convoluted than complex. Who were these authors? When did the two books become one? Who edited?

A better course of action is to consider Job's circumstances. After the Prologue, Job exhausted his ability to cope. He then became frustrated, a volatile emotional state which flared as hostility throughout the Cycles of Dialogue, because God would not talk, his friends should not have talked (13:5), and his relatives would no longer talk to him (19:13–17, 19). After God spoke twice from the whirlwind, Job's bitterness dissipated. The metamorphosis of his temperament hastened in the Epilogue when (1) God censored the friends (42:7–9) and (2) his kin communicated with him again (v. 11).

A better course of action is to recognize Job as a sufferer dealing *honestly* with his circumstances. Unrestrained emotion, especially anger at God, is uncommon today among the faithful, held in check by fear of reproach; to be charged with disrespect, even blasphemy. In the Ancient Near East, however, yelling at God—or the gods—was customary. Two Old Testament examples will suffice.

> **The Ancient Near East is how biblical scholars refer to the Middle East before the New Testament time period.**

First Example: Book of Psalms

True or false: *Every psalm is joy-filled.* After attending the lecture, my students know how to respond: "False!" In the book of Psalms, laments constitute the largest category. A lament "help[s] . . . to express struggles, suffering, or disappointment to the Lord."[50]

> Lord, do not rebuke me in your anger or discipline me in your wrath. Have mercy on me, Lord, for I am faint; heal me, Lord, for my bones are in agony. My soul is in deep anguish. How long, Lord, how long? . . . I am worn out from my groaning; all night long I flood my bed with weeping and drench my couch with tears. (Psalm 6:1–3, 6 NIV)

> Why, O Lord, do you stand far away? Why do you hide yourself in times of trouble? In arrogance the wicked hotly pursue the poor; let them be caught in the schemes that they have devised. (10:1–2 ESV)

> My God, my God, why have you forsaken me? Why are you so far from saving me, from the words of my groaning? O my God, I cry by day, but you do not answer, and by night, but I find no rest. (22:1–2 ESV)

Lord, do not rebuke me in your anger or discipline me in your wrath. Your arrows have pierced me, and your hand has come down on me. Because of your wrath there is no health in my body. (38:1–3 NIV)

Hear my prayer, Lord, listen to my cry for help; do not be deaf to my weeping. I dwell with you as a foreigner, a stranger, as all my ancestors were. Look away from me, that I may enjoy life again before I depart and am no more. (39:12–13 NIV)

If we had forgotten the name of our God or spread out our hands to a foreign god, would not God discover this? For he knows the secrets of the heart. Yet for your sake we are killed all the day long; we are regarded as sheep to be slaughtered. Awake! Why are you sleeping, O Lord? Rouse yourself! Do not reject us forever! Why do you hide your face? Why do you forget our affliction and oppression? For our soul is bowed down to the dust; our belly clings to the ground. Rise up; come to our help! Redeem us for the sake of your steadfast love! (44:20–26 ESV)

Without chapter and verse references, the careful reader could not discern if these words were the psalmist's or Job's.

Second Example: Prophet Jeremiah

As one of the major prophets, the facts about Jeremiah are substantial. His book is fifty-two chapters. It discloses his father's name (Jeremiah 1:1), place of birth (v. 1), time of service (v. 2), call to ministry (vv. 4–19), and marital status (16:1)—for comparison's sake, we know nothing personal about the minor prophets Habakkuk or Malachi.

> The adjective "major" designates Isaiah, Jeremiah, and Ezekiel because their books are considerably longer than the twelve "minor" prophets, Hosea - Malachi. Among the minor prophets, Hosea and Zechariah are the longest books; each one is just fourteen chapters.

Visions, messages, and events pack the book of Jeremiah. Between chapters 11 and 21, five prayers appear: 11:18–12:6; 15:10–12, 15–21; 17:9–10, 14–18; 18:18–23; and 20:7–12, 14–18. Scholars refer to them as the prophet's "Confessions," his candid communications with the Lord, reactions to the widespread harassment that he faced. They qualify as laments.

The fifth confession is an unprecedented outburst of honesty. It begins, "O Lord, you have deceived me, and I was deceived; you are stronger than I, and you have prevailed. I have become a laughingstock all the day; everyone mocks me" (20:7 ESV). The Hebrew verb, translated as "deceive," describes sexual seduction in Exodus 22:16 and Job 31:9. Who else ever accused God of felonious assault?

Honesty Is the Best Policy

After honest rants by Job and Jeremiah, God reacted the same. He didn't slay them or silence them. Jeremiah remained the "go-to" prophet during the late seventh and early sixth centuries BCE. Job received a personal revelation. How many people ever hear God speak audibly?

In 1998, for the first time, I observed how the psalmists, Job, and Jeremiah had protested. Two Mississippi College students invited me to preach at their church in North Jackson, a Church of God of Prophecy; my first—and thus far only—time to preach in a Black church. The evening service began at 5 p.m. and lasted more than two hours! For me, the highlight wasn't my sermon but the scheduled time for testimonies. While a drummer and pianist played, folks throughout the sanctuary spontaneously stood and talked to God while the rest of us listened. Some brimmed with joy; God had been gracious. Some sounded mad, shedding bitter tears about their situation while imploring God to intervene. I sat impressed at the honesty on display that day. Normally, my upbringing would have programmed me to be appalled.

Nine years passed, however, before I tried to do what those worshipers did intuitively. In the summer of 2007, a significant trial impacted our family, directly affecting our eleven-year-old son. My wife and I specifically prayed for God to glorify Himself as our son's advocate; the ordeal was not his fault. We refused to take matters into our own hands; after all, "Those who use the sword will be killed by the sword" (Matthew 26:52 NLT). We prayed, believing that God would promote our son, but, when the summer ended, God did not act as we had pleaded. On a Sunday afternoon, driving north on Interstate 55, I had a heart-to-heart with the Lord. With tears, I expressed to Him my disappointment *and* that I still loved Him. I'm additional evidence that being frank with God isn't life-threatening.

God can handle our honesty. He would rather us turn to Him in rage than turn our backs to Him with a respectful, stifled silence.

Thoughts to Ponder

"One bold message in the Book [sic] of Job is that you can say anything to God. Throw at him your grief, your anger, your doubt, your bitterness, your betrayal, your disappointment—he can absorb them all. As often as not, spiritual giants of the Bible are shown *contending* with God. They prefer to go away limping, like Jacob, rather than to shut God out."[51] (Philip Yancey)

"To be honest and angry with God can be a vital and powerful expression of faith; to do the same with people can bring loneliness and isolation."[52] (Glandion Carney and William Long)

"Cast all your anxiety on him because he cares for you." (1 Peter 5:7 NIV)

"O Lord, you have searched me and known me! You know when I sit down and when I rise up; you discern my thoughts from afar. You search out my path and my lying down and are acquainted with all my ways. Even before a word is on my tongue, behold, O Lord, you know it altogether." (Psalm 139:1-4 ESV)

8

Leaving It Blank

My kids, Anne Marie and Jonathan, are millennials. Recently, I apprised them that they had lost the wonder. Their reaction was puzzlement. A steady diet of my teasing and sarcasm over the years has trained them to assume nothing from me.

"What do you mean, Dad?"

I explained. When my generation was younger, our conversations inevitably led to a baffling question like "*I wonder* if John Wayne was left-handed?" or "*I wonder* which state claims the most Miss Americas?" or "*I wonder* how many World Series the Yankees have lost?" or "*I wonder* if fish have ears?" or "*I wonder* if General Tso ever led an army into battle?" With a smartphone and Google, people today no longer wonder.

Information may be more accessible now, but it is still overrated. Consider three reasons.

1. **Information is useless without context.**

   For example, the answer is forty-two. So what! We need to know why.

2. **Information requires expertise.**

   I'm the son of a cardiologist. In college, I earned an A in anatomy and physiology, a junior-level pre-med course. My experiences equal just enough knowledge to be dangerous and, as a hypochondriac, I can be reckless with self-diagnoses. WebMD should ban me.

3. **Information can be harmful when misapplied.**

   Case in point, consider how Job and his friends processed the two rounds of testing.

"Say What?"

Narrators are fundamental to narrative. They tell the story and interact with readers.[53] In the book of Job, the narrator is unrestricted spatially. He travels freely in the Prologue between heaven and earth as he escorts readers. We, therefore, know why Job suffers. None of the earthly characters ever do, but the words "I don't know" never come out of their mouth. Their lips dripped with confidence.

Speaker: Eliphaz

Behold this, we have investigated it, thus it is; hear it, and know for yourself. (Job 5:27)

Speaker: Job

In truth, I know that this is so, but how can a man be in the right before God? (9:2)

But I have intelligence as well as you; I am not inferior to you. And who does not know such things as these? (12:3)

What you know I also know. I am not inferior to you. (13:2)

Now that I have prepared my case, I know I will be vindicated. (13:18 NIV)

Speaker: Eliphaz

What do you know that we do not know? What do you understand that we do not? (15:9)

Consequently, four scathing rebukes followed.

1. Wisdom Poem: Job 28

The Wisdom Poem immediately follows the Cycles of Dialogue and succinctly critiques every speaker. Verses 12–13 read, "Where can wisdom be found? And where is the place of understanding? Man does not know its value, nor is it found in the land of the living." Paraphrase: The sixteen speeches of Job and his friends lack wisdom.

2. Elihu Speeches: Job 32-37

Elihu chided Job's friends first: "I am young in years and you are old; therefore I was shy and afraid to tell you what I think. I thought age should speak, and increased years should teach wisdom. . . . Behold, I waited for your words, I listened to your reasonings, while you pondered what to say. I even paid close attention to you; Indeed, there was no one who refuted Job, not one of you who answered his words" (32:6–7, 11–12). Before delivering four lengthy speeches to refute Job,

Elihu was blunt, "Behold, let me tell you, you are not right in this, for God is greater than man" (33:12).

Speech 1 (Job 33), Speech 2 (Job 34), Speech 3 (Job 35), and Speech 4 (Job 36-37)

3. Yahweh Speeches: Job 38:1-40:2 and 40:6-41:34

Who is this that darkens counsel by words without knowledge? (38:2)

Will the faultfinder contend with the Almighty? Let him who reproves God answer it (40:2).

4. Epilogue: Job 42:7-17

The Lord said to Eliphaz the Temanite, "My wrath is kindled against you and against your two friends, because you have not spoken of Me what is right" (v. 7).

"Stick to what you know" is great advice. If Job and his friends had known to take it, the book of Job would have been considerably shorter. Less emotional energy would have been spent. Fewer feelings would have been hurt.

God Can Handle Your Blanks

Nature hates a vacuum. Human nature does too.

In Exodus 24, Moses climbed Mount Sinai because God had summoned him: "I will give you the stone tablets with the law and the commandment which I have written for [Israel's] instruction" (v. 12). Accompanied by Joshua, Moses stayed forty days and forty nights. The Israelites below eventually lost patience, assuming the worst about Moses's absence. Consequently, they implored Aaron,

"Come, make us a god who will go before us; as for this Moses, the man who brought us up from the land of Egypt, we do not know what has become of him" (32:1). A national tragedy followed: Israel's sin provoked judgment. About three thousand men perished (vv. 25–28).

Uncertainty understandably causes anxiety. Unfortunately, anxiety does not inspire good decision-making. The anxious mind settles for anything because the facts, whether few or many, are not enough. Fortunately, faith is also an option when one faces the unknown; defined as "the substance of things hoped for, the evidence of things not seen" (Hebrews 11:1 KJV).

During the fall of 2013, life blindsided my family. Our daughter manifested manic depression. She was twenty years old, a college junior, and a math major.

We all endured a lot of lows; each of us processed them differently. I recall being awakened several nights by gnawing questions.

- Can Anne Marie finish this semester?
- Will her medications, despite their side-effects, work?
- What kind of future does she have? Graduation? Marriage? Career? Kids?
- Will we ever see the "old" Anne Marie again?

I resolved not to speculate or to extrapolate, realizing that I was as unqualified to handle "what ifs" as I was unqualified to handle a routine "what." In those torturous moments, I opted to pray believing, but the only prayer that I could muster was "God, help us" over and over. Although not eloquent, it was effective. I received an incomprehensible peace (Philippians 4:6–7) that lulled me back to sleep every time.

Thoughts to Ponder

"Job seeks knowledge because we all seek knowledge; the quest for knowledge and rational explanation is insatiable. This quest is our limited attempt to make the world comprehensible, to feel at home in the world, to feel that we not only have a role to play in this unpredictable human drama but also that we may comprehend at least a few of the ways that the world works."[54] (Glandion Carney and William Long)

"You asked, 'Who is this who conceals my counsel with ignorance?' Surely I spoke about things I did not understand, things too wondrous for me to know.'" (Job 42:3 CSB)

"Trust in the Lord with all your heart, and do not rely on your own understanding; in all your ways know him, and he will make your paths straight." (Proverbs 3:5-6 CSB)

"When I try, I fail. When I trust, He succeeds."[55] (Ryan McGuyre, Women's Volleyball Coach at Baylor University)

9

Waiting When God Is Silent

In January 1966, a remixed version of "The Sound of Silence," Simon and Garfunkel's first hit, topped the *Billboard* Hot 100. The single originally appeared on side one of the duo's debut album, which flopped, and in turn convinced Simon and Garfunkel to part ways. Consequently, the iconic song's eventual success rescued two fledgling careers.[56] On February 14, 1966, "The Sound of Silence" earned RIAA gold certification.[57]

Is silence always "golden"? Context determines how one answers the question. Parents savor peace and quiet. "Dead air," on the other hand, would alarm a radio or television producer. Librarians oppose talking; interviewers, of course, do not. Rests provide needed transitions for a melody to develop. Meanwhile, prosecutors neither need nor want defendants to plead the Fifth.

Silence is an appropriate response before God.

> Do not be hasty in word or impulsive in thought to bring up a matter in the presence of God. For God is in

heaven and you are on the earth; therefore let your words be few. (Ecclesiastes 5:2)

The Lord is in His holy temple. Let all the earth be silent before Him. (Habakkuk 2:20)

Be silent before the Lord God! For the day of the Lord is near. (Zephaniah 1:7)

Be silent, all flesh, before the Lord; for He is aroused from His holy habitation. (Zechariah 2:13)

For God's followers, however, His silence can be problematic.[58]

But I cry to you for help, Lord; in the morning my prayer comes before you. Why, Lord, do you reject me and hide your face from me? (Psalm 88:13–14 NIV)

Your sacred cities have become a wasteland; even Zion is a wasteland, Jerusalem a desolation. Our holy and glorious temple, where our ancestors praised you, has been burned with fire, and all that we treasured lies in ruins. After all this, Lord, will you hold yourself back? Will you keep silent and punish us beyond measure? (Isaiah 64:10–12 NIV)

Why are you silent while the wicked swallow up those more righteous than themselves? (Habakkuk 1:13 NIV)

God's silence is not His unwillingness to communicate. He reveals Himself in creation (Psalm 19:1–6; Romans 1:18–20). He answers prayer (Jeremiah 33:3; Matthew 7:7–8; 21:22; 1 John 5:14). He has recorded His personal words—namely, the Bible—for all people.

God's silence is what humans occasionally perceive to be reality, a perception triggered by our unmet expectations—when God should have responded and how He should have responded. Such silence exacerbated Job's despair.

Why do you hide your face and count me as your enemy? (Job 13:24 ESV)

I cry to you for help and you do not answer me; I stand, and you only look at me. You have turned cruel to me; with the might of your hand you persecute me. You lift me up on the wind; you make me ride on it, and you toss me about in the roar of the storm. For I know that you will bring me to death and to the house appointed for all living. (30:20–23 ESV)

Oh that I had one to hear me! (31:35)

"Talk to Me!"

In the book of Job, God is not the most talkative character. That distinction belongs to Job. God is talked about more than anyone else, the only character mentioned in every chapter, but His own words, measured by chapter and verse, are less than Job's or Elihu's.

How does one coax a deity to speak? Job resorted to extreme measures. He sued God.[59]

Now that I have prepared my case, I know I will be vindicated. Can anyone bring charges against me? If so, I will be silent and die. (13:18–19 NIV)

Today also my complaint is bitter; my hand is heavy on account of my groaning. Oh, that I knew where I might find him, that I might come even to his seat! I would lay my case before him and fill my mouth with arguments. I would know what he would answer me and understand what he would say to me. Would he contend with me in the greatness of his power? No, he would pay attention to me. There an upright man could argue with him, and I would be acquitted forever by my judge. (23:2–7 ESV)

His lawsuit leveled two charges.
- God abuses His omnipotence (9:5–12, 19; 10:8–9, 16; 12:9–10, 14–15, 16–21, 23–25; 14:1–6, 18–22; 23:6)
- God ignores wickedness (9:24; 10:3; 12:6; 21:7–26, 29–33; 24:1–17)

The rest of the story reveals that Job had grossly misjudged God. He assumed that God could be forced to act, that He would need to defend Himself. As time passed, however, heaven's deafening silence forced Job to make an unprecedented Oath of Innocence (chap. 31, my translations below). It dared God to contest him, to convict him, and to curse him. As if Job hadn't suffered enough!

If I walked with deception and my foot hastened towards deceit, let him weigh me in just scales. May God know my integrity. (31:5–6)

If my step deviated from the way or my heart followed my eyes or a blemish clung to my hands, let me sow but another eat and let my produce be rooted up. (vv. 7–8)

If my heart was enticed because of a woman and I lay in wait by the doorway of my friend, let my wife grind for another man and let others bow down over her. (vv. 9–10)

If I withheld from the poor their longing or exhausted the tears of a widow or ate my morsel alone, not allowing an orphan to eat from it—since my youth, I was like a father to the orphan growing up. From the womb of my mother, I led the widow—if I saw someone perishing without clothing or no covering for a needy person; if his loins did not bless me, warming themselves with a fleece from my lambs; if I shook my hand at the orphan when

I perceived my support in the gate, let my shoulder blade fall from its shoulder and let my arm be broken from the shoulder joint. (vv. 16–22)

If my land cried out against me and its furrows wept together, if I consumed its strength without paying, if I suffocated the life of its owners, let briars come forth instead of wheat, stinking weeds instead of barley. (vv. 38–40)

After the Oath of Innocence, the narrator announced, "The words of Job are ended" (v. 40). Was it a "drop the mic" moment? Job had been gloating.

Behold, here is my signature; let the Almighty answer me! And the indictment which my adversary has written, surely I would carry it on my shoulder; I would bind it to myself like a crown. I would declare to Him the number of my steps; like a prince I would approach Him. (vv. 35–37)

Job reckoned that he had outmaneuvered God. Hence, the pending results of his tactics had emboldened him.

Outcome #1
If God did respond, even if it were a rebuttal, Job would have coerced it.
Assessment: Victory for Job

Outcome #2
If God did not respond, failing to show up at all, Job could claim exoneration.
Assessment: Victory for Job

What actually happened next shocked Job. A young man named Elihu delivered four lengthy speeches.

Why Is God Silent?

Every semester, from fall 2004 to spring 2021, only one of my classes could evaluate me—one of the perks of tenure. Mississippi College students provide feedback in two forms: (1) Quantitative: Rating Scale of 1–5 (1 being the lowest, 5 being the highest) and (2) Qualitative: "Comments." What used to be a #2 pencil and two forms is now online.

The "Comments" section solicits opinions by asking respondents two questions: (1) What did you like best about this class? and (2) Would you recommend any changes? Of course, my eyes find the negative comments first. Reading what students write is a job hazard that takes me months to conjure enough courage. Sometimes, I learn something. Sometimes, the comments are contradictory.

Style of Teaching
- "somewhat fast"
- "maybe a little faster paced so we could get thru the whole Old Testament"

Assessment of Learning
- "test shorter or multiple choice"
- "I recommend that the teacher give more test [sic]."
- "potentially more written assignments and less testing"
- "I would recommend quizzes, maybe weekly, to help the learning process & provide more grades to help students."
- "no paper"

Length of Course
- "I would decrease class time."

- "The only change that I recommend regarding this class is time. The time isn't long enough."
- "Longer class times. The OT is a long work."

If God distributed a "Comment" sheet, His communication style would be flagged. Our demand for answers inevitably collides with His will not to answer. In those conflicts, God always prevails. Not even close! "Woe to the one who quarrels with his Maker—an earthenware vessel among the vessels of earth! Will the clay say to the potter, 'What are you doing?'" (Isaiah 45:9)

God does prefer to work subtly, a lesson that Elijah saw, felt, and heard. On Mount Carmel, fire fell from the sky because the prophet had prayed (1 Kings 18:37–38). Later, on Mount Horeb, God tempered Elijah's expectations.

> So He said, "Go forth, and stand on the mountain before the Lord." And behold, the Lord was passing by! And a great and strong wind was rending the mountains and breaking in pieces the rocks before the Lord; but the Lord was not in the wind. And after the wind an earthquake, but the Lord was not in the earthquake. And after the earthquake a fire, but the Lord was not in the fire; and after the fire a sound of a gentle blowing. (19:11–12)

Horeb is another name for Sinai, the mountain of God (Exodus 3:1–5; Deuteronomy 1:6–8; 4:10–18; 5:1–21; 1 Kings 8:6–9; 2 Chronicles 5:7–10; Psalm 106:19–22; Malachi 4:4).

The last three Hebrew words in 1 Kings 19:12 are not easy to render. Compare three English possibilities.

- a sound of a gentle blowing (NASB)
- a still, small voice (KJV, NKJV)

- a gentle whisper (NIV)

Despite the differences, the meaning is clear: God can be quiet.

Talk is cheap whereas timing is critical, which is why Ecclesiastes specifies "a time to be silent, and a time to speak" (3:7). Because silence is now sporadic, twenty-first-century folk have not developed an appetite for it. My fellow Gen Xers, however, can remember when television stations signed off every night. No twenty-four-hour news cycles. My fellow Gen Xers can remember life before internet, e-mail, and social media. We functioned with less communication, thus less information.

Timing matters to God. "He has made everything beautiful in its time" (v. 11). "Timely," therefore, describes His actions, like when and what to say. In the meantime, He easily resists the impassioned plea or the impudent demand to answer. He has nothing to prove, no need to impress. He isn't insecure.

God uses periods of silence as invaluable teachable moments to grow our faith and to improve our discernment; that we might trust without seeing (2 Corinthians 5:7) and discern without hearing. Anyone can believe when fire falls from the sky (1 Kings 18:38–39).

How to Cope When God Is Silent

God's silence defines His "waiting room," a place—metaphorically speaking—that His followers dread. Though waiting expends no calories, it can be emotionally draining when we spend the time worrying rather than trusting and praying. Faith quashes the hysteric assumption that God's silence is apathy, inactivity, or absence. Prayer keeps the lines of communication open; attuning our attention when He does answer. He always does; for Job, unlike Elijah, out of a whirlwind (Job 38:1–40:2; 40:6–41:34).

Thoughts to Ponder

"Although you say you do not see Him, yet justice is before Him, and you must wait for Him." (Job 35:14 NKJV)

"Why do you say, O Jacob, and speak, O Israel, 'My way is hidden from the Lord, and my right is disregarded by my God?' Have you not known? Have you not heard? The Lord is the everlasting God, the Creator of the ends of the earth. He does not faint or grow weary; his understanding is unsearchable. He gives power to the faint, and to him who has no might he increases strength. Even youths shall faint and be weary, and young men shall fall exhausted; but they who wait for the Lord shall renew their strength; they shall mount up with wings like eagles; they shall run and not be weary; they shall walk and not faint." (Isaiah 40:27-31 ESV)

"The kind of faith God values seems to develop best when everything fuzzes over, when God stays silent, when the fog rolls in."[60] (Philip Yancey)

"Because you have seen Me, have you believed? Blessed are they who did not see, and yet believed." (John 20:29)

10

Welcoming God's Imperceptible Presence

In 1949, English author George Orwell published *1984*. He foresaw a bleak future when totalitarian government would use technology to terrorize its citizens. Winston Smith, the novel's main character, lives in Oceania. In his flat, a telescreen monitors him, the government's eyes and ears; it cannot be turned off. Posters outside everywhere remind him, "Big Brother is watching."

During Round One of the Cycles of Dialogue (Job 4–14), Job, responding to Eliphaz, railed against God.

> Therefore I will not restrain my mouth; I will speak in the anguish of my spirit; I will complain in the bitterness of my soul. Am I the sea, or a sea monster, that you set a guard over me? When I say, "My bed will comfort me, my couch will ease my complaint," then you scare me with dreams and terrify me with visions, so that I would choose

strangling and death rather than my bones. I loathe my life; I would not live forever. Leave me alone, for my days are a breath. What is man, that you make so much of him, and that you set your heart on him, visit him every morning and test him every moment? How long will you not look away from me, nor leave me alone till I swallow my spit? If I sin, what do I do to you, you watcher of mankind? Why have you made me your mark? Why have I become a burden to you? Why do you not pardon my transgression and take away my iniquity? For now I shall lie in the earth; you will seek me, but I shall not be. (7:11–21 ESV)

The combination of God's silence and God's presence had become unbearable.

Omnipresence

Systematic theologians have categorized the attributes of God.[61] For example:

Absolute and Relative

Absolute attributes are qualities that God possessed eternally before creation. Relative attributes manifest through God's relationships with time and space.

Communicable and Incommunicable

Communicable attributes can be qualities that human beings possess. Incommunicable attributes are unique to God.

Natural and Moral

Natural attributes are God's superlatives, such as His knowledge and power. Moral attributes relate to the concept of rightness in human contexts.

According to these lists, omnipresence is relative, incommunicable, and natural.

Omnipresence means that God is everywhere always. Time and space do not restrict Him. Omnipresence relates to His immanence, the fact that He is near and accessible (Deuteronomy 4:7; Jeremiah 29:13). Psalm 139 offers the best description of omnipresence.

O Lord, you have searched me and known me! You know when I sit down and when I rise up; you discern my thoughts from afar. You search out my path and my lying down and are acquainted with all my ways. Even before a word is on my tongue, behold, O Lord, you know it altogether. You hem me in, behind and before, and lay your hand upon me. Such knowledge is too wonderful for me; it is high; I cannot attain it. Where shall I go from your Spirit? Or where shall I flee from your presence? If I ascend to heaven, you are there! If I make my bed in Sheol, you are there! If I take the wings of the morning and dwell in the uttermost parts of the sea, even there your hand shall lead me, and your right hand shall hold me. If I say, "Surely the darkness shall cover me, and the light around me be night," even the darkness is not dark to you; the night is bright as the day, for darkness is as light with you. (vv. 1–12 ESV)

David's words in verse 6 echo Job's worshipful response after Yahweh's second speech: "Such knowledge is too wonderful for me" (compare to Job 42:3).

What moved David to praise God, however, had pushed Job, during the Cycles of Dialogue, to protest. The reason was that Job blamed God for his suffering (Job 9:17–18; 19:21–22; 23:16). He described God as a warrior attacking him (6:4; 16:12–14; 19:8–

12) or a hunter stalking him (10:16–17; 16:7–9; 19:6). God's presence thus threatened Job.

The terrors of God are arrayed against me. (6:4)

Withdraw your hand far from me, and stop frightening me with your terrors. (13:21 NIV; see also 6:9 and 23:2)

God was "Big Brother."

Are not my days few? Then cease, and leave me alone, that I may find a little cheer before I go—and I shall not return—to the land of darkness and deep shadow, the land of gloom like thick darkness, like deep shadow without any order, where light is as thick darkness. (10:20–22 ESV)

For you write bitter things against me and make me inherit the iniquities of my youth. You put my feet in the stocks and watch all my paths; you set a limit for the soles of my feet. (13:26–27 ESV; see also 14:3, 6; 31:4)

Surely now God has worn me out; he has made desolate all my company. And he has shriveled me up, which is a witness against me, and my leanness has risen up against me; it testifies to my face. He has torn me in his wrath and hated me; he has gnashed his teeth at me; my adversary sharpens his eyes against me. (16:7–9 ESV)

El Shaddai Is Not a Shadow

Edward Snowden stumbled upon the facts of George Orwell's fiction. In 2013, the former Dell employee, assigned to the National Security Agency (NSA), leaked hundreds of thousands of classified documents that unmasked the NSA's unwarranted surveillance of millions of innocent Americans.[62] A spy film can be entertaining, but the invasion of one's privacy is not. The American Civil Liberties Union contends that the documents prove that the Bush and Obama administrations violated the Fourth Amendment.[63]

> *Shaddai*, translated "Almighty" occurs forty-eight times in the Old Testament and thirty-one times in the book of Job.

In the movies, spies wear a trench coat and sunglasses (disguise) and lurk in the shadows (distance). If God were to eavesdrop, His invisibility would be better than any disguise, to be everywhere (no distance) undetected.

Job could not call God a "snoop." The words "spy" and "surveillance" do not exist in biblical Hebrew, but Job did whine that God was unruly as Creator, that His abuses outweighed His wisdom, and that His invisibility enhanced His invincibility.

Wise in heart and mighty in strength, who has defied Him without harm? It is God who removes the mountains, they know not how, when He overturns them in His anger; who shakes the earth out of its place, and its pillars tremble; who commands the sun not to shine, and sets a seal upon the stars; who alone stretches out the heavens, and tramples down the waves of the sea; who makes the Bear, Orion, and the Pleiades, and the chambers of the south; who does great things, unfathomable, and wondrous works without number. Were He to pass by me, I would not see Him; were He to move past me, I would not perceive Him. (9:4–11; see also 12:13–25)

Behold, I go forward but He is not there, and backward, but I cannot perceive Him; when He acts on the left, I cannot behold Him; He turns on the right, I cannot see Him. (23:8–9)

In His first speech from the whirlwind, God rebutted Job, citing sufficient examples of His beneficial knowledge and benevolent presence.

Beneficial Knowledge

As Creator, God laid well the earth's foundation (38:4–7). His priority then became managing the planet, a to-do list that includes restraining the vast sea (vv. 8–11), ordering both day and night (vv. 12–15, 19–21), and controlling the weather (vv. 22–30, 34–38). Caring for the planet also transcends it: God positions every star (vv. 31–33).

Benevolent Presence

Animals fear humans (Genesis 9:1–2) but not their Creator. He feeds lions and ravens (Job 38:39–41). Like an expectant father, He anticipates the birth of mountain goats and deer (39:1–4). He freed the donkey to roam in a better home (vv. 5–8) and instructs the eagle where best to nest (vv. 27–30). The folly of an ostrich and the fearlessness of a horse captivate Him (vv. 13–25).

God's incontrovertible testimony overwhelmed Job. Consequently, he praised the Creator like David did: "I have uttered what I did not understand, things too wonderful for me, which I did not know" (42:3 ESV; compare to Psalm 139:6).

El Shaddai Is God with Us (Immanuel)

Psalms, being poetry, employs a variety of imagery, both personal and impersonal, to describe God. "Redeemer" (19:14), "shepherd" (23:1), or "deliverer" (144:2) would be personal imagery. "Rock" (18:2), "light" (27:1), or "shield" (119:14) would be impersonal imagery.

Neither Psalms nor the rest of Scripture depicts God as a "shadow." The reasons are obvious. First, a shadow is passive. God, on the other hand, is active being, the ultimate cause.[64] At the burning bush, He identified Himself as "I AM THAT I AM" (Exodus 3:14), sovereign over the present where all history happens. Nothing takes place in the past (what the present used to be) or the future (what the present will be). Second, a shadow disappears in the dark. God, on the other hand, never abandons us during life's darkest moments. Peter, addressing Gentile Christians facing persecution, could assure them, "If you are insulted for the name of Christ, you are blessed, *because the Spirit of glory and of God rests upon you*" (1 Peter 4:14 ESV, italics mine).

Holocaust survivor Elie Wiesel, in his memoir *Night*, recounts the hanging of a young boy charged with sabotage. The SS guards forced every prisoner to watch the execution.

> The three condemned prisoners together stepped onto the chairs. In unison, the nooses were placed around their necks.
>
> "Long live liberty!" shouted the two men.
>
> But the boy was silent.
>
> "Where is merciful God, where is He?" someone behind me was asking.
>
> At the signal, the three chairs were tipped over.
>
> Total silence in the camp. On the horizon, the sun was setting.
>
> "Caps off!" screamed the *Lagerälteste*. His voice quivered. As for the rest of us, we were weeping. . . .
>
> Then came the march past the victims. The two men were no longer alive. Their tongues were hanging out, swollen and bluish. But the third rope was still moving: the child, too light, was still breathing . . .

And so he remained for more than half an hour, lingering between life and death, writhing before our eyes. And we were forced to look at him at close range. He was still alive when I passed him. His tongue was still red, his eyes not yet extinguished.

Behind me, I heard the same man asking:

"For God's sake, where is God?"

And from within me, I heard a voice answer:

"Where He is? This is where—hanging here from this gallows . . ."[65]

God doesn't "shadow" us like a spy, staying a safe distance away; why, from the darkness, the prophet Micah could assert, "As for me, I will watch expectantly for the Lord; I will wait for the God of my salvation. My God will hear me. Do not rejoice over me, O my enemy. Though I fall I will rise; though I dwell in darkness, the Lord is a light for me" (Micah 7:7–8).

Thoughts to Ponder

"For [God] looks to the ends of the earth, and sees everything under the heavens." (Job 28:24)

"For [God's] eyes are upon the ways of a man, and He sees all his steps." (Job 34:21)

"For the eyes of Yahweh roam throughout the earth to show Himself strong for those whose hearts are completely His." (2 Chronicles 16:9 HCSB)

"Oh that I were as in months gone by, as in the days when God watched over me; when His lamp shone over my head, and by His light I walked through darkness." (Job 29:2-3)

"Even though I walk through the valley of the shadow of death, I will fear no evil, for you are with me; your rod and your staff, they comfort me." (Psalm 23:4 ESV)

11

Rejecting Pessimism:
A Box without God

T he devout, regardless of religion, merit the label "believers." What one believes religiously is theology. A theological extreme that besets believers is dogmatism: "pos-
itiveness in assertion of opinion especially when unwarranted or
arrogant."[66] Eliphaz, Bildad, or Zophar could have been the poster
child for dogmatism. They put God in a theological box, the doctrine of divine retribution.

The devout can doubt too. Exhibit A: John the Baptist. He
would have been an unlikely example, based upon the highlights
of his résumé.

- fulfillment of Old Testament prophecies in Isaiah (such
  as 40:1–3) and Malachi (see 3:1; 4:5–6)
- filled with the Holy Spirit *before* birth (Luke 1:15)
- "forerunner" (v. 17) for the long-awaited Messiah
- "among those born of women, there is no one greater"
  (7:28), according to Jesus

Despair, however, led John to doubt. He had been unjustly jailed by Antipas for proclaiming the truth. When the prison stay became unbearable, John dispatched two of his disciples. Their mission was to ask Jesus one question, "Are You the Expected One, or do we look for someone else?" (7:18–20). John actually wondered if he had been mistaken about the Messiah's identity. The "real" Lamb of God (John 1:29) would not let His forerunner rot in custody, right?

The road named "Doubt" winds through pessimism and skepticism and ends at cynicism. The cynic, unlike the believer, couldn't care less. During the Cycles of Dialogue, despair drove Job to pessimism but no farther because God intervened, contacting him from the whirlwind.

Heart Condition

My father is a doctor who didn't want to retire. He's eighty-four. For most of his career, he was a cardiologist. I am biased, but one would have been hard-pressed to find a better physician. I've told friends and strangers, "My dad's the best doctor that I hope you never need!"

My father's primary task was to diagnose. The electrocardiogram, echocardiogram, stress test, and catheterization were his tools. His patients typically had hypertension, high cholesterol, clogged arteries, or an abnormal heartbeat. Dad never treated what the Bible calls a melting heart, heavy heart, sad heart, or heart loss.

I am poured out like water, and all my bones are out of joint; my heart is like wax; it is melted within me. (Psalm 22:14)

Anxiety in the heart of a man weighs it down, but a good word makes it glad. (Proverbs 12:25)

A joyful heart makes a cheerful face, but when the heart is sad, the spirit is broken. (Proverbs 15:13)

We do not lose heart, but though our outer man is decaying, yet our inner man is being renewed day by day. (2 Corinthians 4:16)

During Round Three of the Cycles of Dialogue, Job alleged, "God has made my heart faint; the Almighty has terrified me" (Job 23:16 ESV). Job's self-diagnosis occurred during a roller-coaster ride between hope and despair.

When the theological argument with his friends began, Job's emotions raged, sorrowful as well as hopeful. His hope manifested as a confidence of innocence and an expectation of vindication.

Round One: Chapters 4-14

Oh that my request might come to pass, and that God would grant my longing! Would that God were willing to crush me; that He would loose His hand and cut me off! But it is still my consolation, and I rejoice in unsparing pain, that I have not denied the words of the Holy One. (6:8–10)

I loathe my life; I will give free utterance to my complaint; I will speak in the bitterness of my soul. (10:1 ESV; see also 7:11)

Although you know I am not guilty, no one can rescue me from your power. (10:7 NLT)

Now that I have prepared my case, I know I will be vindicated. (13:18 NIV)

Oh that you would hide me in Sheol, that you would conceal me until your wrath be past, that you would appoint me a set time, and remember me! If a man dies, shall he live again? All the days of my service I would wait, till my renewal should come. You would call, and I would answer you; you would long for the work of your hands. (14:13–15 ESV)

Each round took its toll. As a result, Job became more sorrowful than hopeful.

Round Two: Chapters 15-21

I have sewed sackcloth over my skin, and thrust my horn in the dust. My face is flushed with weeping, and deep darkness is on my eyelids, although there is no violence in my hands, and my prayer is pure. (16:15–17)

My eye has also grown dim because of grief, and all my members are as a shadow. (17:7)

Have mercy on me, my friends, have mercy, for God's hand has struck me. (19:21 HCSB)

For I know that my Redeemer lives, and at the last he will stand upon the earth. And after my skin has been thus destroyed, yet in my flesh I shall see God, whom I shall see for myself, and my eyes shall behold, and not another. My heart faints within me! (19:25–27 ESV)

Round Three: Chapters 22-27

I am not silenced because of the darkness, nor because thick darkness covers my face. (23:17 ESV)

As God lives, who has taken away my right, and the Almighty, who has embittered my soul, for as long as life is in me, and the breath of God is in my nostrils, my lips certainly will not speak unjustly, nor will my tongue mutter deceit. Far be it from me that I should declare you right; till I die I will not put away my integrity from me. I hold fast my righteousness and will not let it go. My heart does not reproach any of my days. (27:2–6)

Job's final speech, his Second Monologue (chaps. 29–31), reveals the depth of his angst.

I cry to you for help and you do not answer me; I stand, and you only look at me. You have turned cruel to me; with the might of your hand you persecute me. You lift me up on the wind; you make me ride on it, and you toss me about in the roar of the storm. For I know that you will bring me to death and to the house appointed for all living. (30:20–23 ESV)

When I expected good, then evil came; when I waited for light, then darkness came. I am seething within, and cannot relax; days of affliction confront me. I go about mourning without comfort; I stand up in the assembly and cry out for help. I have become a brother to jackals and a companion of ostriches. My skin turns black on me, and my bones burn with fever. Therefore my harp is turned to mourning, and my flute to the sound of those who weep. (30:26–31)

Spiritual Problem

Pessimism is "an inclination to emphasize adverse aspects, conditions, and possibilities or to expect the worst possible outcome."[67] Job had had several pessimistic outbursts before his "harp . . . turned to mourning, and . . . flute to the sound of those who weep" (30:31).

Round One: Chapters 4-14

What is my strength, that I should wait? And what is my end, that I should endure? Is my strength the strength of stones, or is my flesh bronze? Is it that my help is not within me, and that deliverance is driven from me? (6:11–13)

Why did you bring me out from the womb? Would that I had died before any eye had seen me and were as though I had not been, carried from the womb to the grave. Are not my days few? Then cease, and leave me alone, that I may find a little cheer before I go—and I shall not return—to the land of darkness and deep shadow, the land of gloom like thick darkness, like deep shadow without any order, where light is as thick darkness. (10:18–22 ESV)

Round Two: Chapter 15-21

My friends are my scoffers; my eye weeps to God. O that a man might plead with God as a man with his neighbor! For when a few years are past, I shall go the way of no return. (16:20–22)

My days are past, my plans are torn apart, even the wishes of my heart. They make night into day, saying, "The light is near," in the presence of darkness. If I look for Sheol as my home, I make my bed in the darkness; if I call to the pit, "You are my father"; to the worm, "my mother and my sister"; where now is my hope? And who regards my hope? Will it go down with me to Sheol? Shall we together go down into the dust? (17:11–16)

The future depressed Job because he blamed God. He believed that the answer to his problem was the problem. Of course, he was wrong.

Pessimism for the rest of us, if we don't blame God, still disregards God. It boxes Him out of the present and the future. To think the worst, therefore, is worse than pretending to be clairvoyant; i.e., presuming to know what will happen. To think the worst is to conclude that God won't (because He doesn't care) or can't change one's situation. Long live status quo! Why bother to pray?

Our society has practiced and perfected pessimism. Recall its slogans, just the ones without a four-letter word.

- "Same old same old."
- "Déjà vu all over again."
- "Been there, done that."

In contrast, consider the realism of a psalmist. "This is the day which the Lord has made; let us rejoice and be glad in it" (Psalm 118:24). Realism, if it really is reality-based, must be God-centered.

The next-to-last Hebrew verb in Psalm 118:24 presents a fabulous image. Translated "to rejoice," its root meaning is "to circle around," denoting "enthusiastic expressions of joy,"[68] like the spectacle of unbridled exuberance after a sports team has won the championship. Is that your reaction when the alarm harshly interrupts your sleep? Anyone can celebrate *after* something wonderful happens. To celebrate at daybreak, *before* anything substantive occurs, is lunacy to the world but a logical response for us who personally know the God of the universe. He has no limitations. He delivers "future and a hope" (Jeremiah 29:11).

Thoughts to Ponder

"I know that you can do anything and no plan of yours can be thwarted." (Job 42:2 CSB)

"With men it is impossible but with God all things are possible." (Matthew 19:18)

"Now to Him who is able to do exceeding abundantly beyond all that we ask or think, according to the power that works within us." (Ephesians 3:20)

12

Contending with Criticism

ustralian actor Hugh Jackman played P. T. Barnum in *The Greatest Showman*. The 2017 movie features an on-going clash between Barnum, the entertainer and entrepreneur, and James Gordon Bennett, a theater critic. Bennett wrote for *The New York Herald*. His columns disparaged Barnum's show, calling it a "circus." He chose adjectives like "shame of the city," "criminal," and "degrading." He referred to P. T. Barnum as "a purveyor of the offensive and indecent."

Three face-to-face exchanges between the two men were brief but not much better.

Excerpt: First Conversation

Bennett: "Tell me, Mr. Barnum, does it bother you that everything you're selling is fake?"

Barnum: "Do these smiles seem fake? It doesn't matter where they come from. The joy is real."

Bennett: "So, you are a philanthropist?"

Barnum: "Well, hyperbole isn't the worst crime. Men suffer more from imagining too little than too much."

Bennett: "The creed of a true fraud."

Barnum: "Mr. Bennett, when was the last time you smiled or had a good laugh? Like a real laugh? A theater critic who can't find joy in the theater. Now who's a fraud?"

Excerpt: Second Conversation

Barnum: "You really are better on the page, Mr. Bennett, hard as that is to believe."

Excerpt: Third Conversation

Bennett: "I never liked your show. But I always thought the people did. . . . Mind you, I wouldn't call it art. . . but . . . another critic might have even called it a celebration of humanity."[69]

The movie depicts Barnum unable to fully enjoy his remarkable rags-to-riches life. One reason is his father-in-law. Another reason is Bennett, which is why a supporter asked Barnum, "What do you care what Bennett thinks?"

Job cared too much about what people said and how they treated him. Eliphaz, Bildad, and Zophar were his chief critics. He couldn't ignore their words, venting, "If only you would be altogether silent! For you, that would be wisdom" (Job 13:5 NIV). As a result, Job became paranoid.

Diagnosis: Paranoia

Paranoia can be a separate disorder or associated with schizophrenia. "A person with a paranoid disorder is troubled by persistent persecutory delusions or by delusional jealousy. . . . unlike the paranoid schizophrenic, he or she has no thought disorder, no hallucinations, and no bizarre delusions, such as the belief that thoughts are being broadcast."[70]

The term "paranoia" is relatively new, ca. 1811.[71] The behavior itself is not. Case in point, Israel's first king. Saul exhibited an array of abnormal behaviors during his demise, besides paranoia: fits (1 Samuel 16:14–23; 18:10–11; 19:9–10), obsession (hunting David, 19:18–26:25), and Hebephrenia; i.e., inappropriate expression of emotions (chap. 24, especially v. 16). First Samuel 22 records a textbook example of paranoia when the king chastised his advisors.

Hear now, O Benjamites! Will the son of Jesse also give to all of you fields and vineyards? Will he make you all commanders of thousands and commanders of hundreds? For all of you have conspired against me so that there is no one who discloses to me when my son makes a covenant with the son of Jesse, and there is none of you who is sorry for me or discloses to me that my son has stirred up my servant against me to lie in ambush, as it is this day. (vv. 7–8)

Job sounded like Saul.

God has made my brothers my enemies, and my friends have become strangers. My relatives have gone away, and my friends have forgotten me. My guests and my female servants treat me like a stranger; they look at me as if I were a foreigner. I call for my servant, but he does not answer, even when I beg him with my own mouth. My wife can't stand my breath, and my own family dislikes me. Even the little boys hate me and talk about me when I leave. All my close friends hate me; even those I love have turned against me. (Job 19:13–19 NCV)

But now they mock me, men younger than I. . . . And now those young men mock me in song; I have become a byword among them. They detest me and keep their distance; they do not hesitate to spit in my face. Now that God has unstrung my bow and afflicted me, they throw off restraint in my presence. On my right the tribe attacks; they lay snares for my feet, they build their siege ramps against me. They break up my road; they succeed in destroying me. "No one can help him," they say. They advance as through a gaping breach; amid the ruins they come rolling in. Terrors overwhelm me; my dignity is driven away as by the wind, my safety vanishes like a cloud. (30:1, 9–15 NIV)

John Wooden won ten national championships at UCLA. He cautioned, "If you listen to too much criticism it will hurt your coaching and if you listen to too much praise it will hurt your coaching."[72] I still regret reading my first anonymous letter, slipped into my briefcase at an out-of-town retreat center where I had led a Bible study on Job. It really rattled my self-confidence. I also wasted energy, trying to figure out who had wielded the poison pen; a coward who presumed to know me and love me constructively.

Criticism thins one's skin and tricks one's senses; consequently, several nitpickers can sound like a multitude or, worse, a mob. Sparring with his critics affected Job's ability to cope, thus exacerbating his suffering.

Living Faster than Criticism

American lecturer, publisher, editor, and essayist Elbert Hubbard recommended, "To escape criticism—do nothing, say nothing, be nothing."[73] Hubbard's suggestion, whether serious or sarcastic, should be rejected because criticism is inescapable. It exempts no one, living or deceased, young or old, active or idle, kind or cruel, flawed or perfect. Jesus Himself endured vicious personal attacks. His critics, the Jewish religious leadership, even condemned Him. One of Jesus's disciples recollected, "Christ also suffered for you, leaving you an example for you to follow in His steps, who committed no sin, nor was any deceit found in His mouth; and while being reviled, He did not revile in return; while suffering, He uttered no threats, but kept entrusting Himself to Him who judges righteously" (1 Peter 2:21–23). The Greek verb translated "being reviled" is a present tense participle, thus depicting continuous action, signifying an ongoing assault. It denotes the use of "vile and abusive language."[74]

How did the "man of sorrows" (Isaiah 53:2) cope? Jesus focused on His mission. It was His food (John 4:34). Luke writes, "He made a firm resolve (lit., set his face) to go to Jerusalem" (Luke 9:51). There, on a cross, while being jeered, Jesus declared, "It is finished" (John 19:30). Mission accomplished!

If unjust criticism is inevitable, then be maligned for doing what is right, pursuing God wholeheartedly, neither fearful nor regretful. Peter makes a similar argument in regard to religious persecution (see 1 Peter 2:12; 3:16–17; 4:19). Responding to critics empowers them, enabling them to sidetrack us. Focusing on God's will forces them to react (being passive) rather than to set the agenda.

Thoughts to Ponder

"A critic is a legless man who teaches running."[75] (American novelist and dramatist Channing Pollock)

"Pay no attention to what the critics say; no statue has ever been put up to a critic."[76] (Finnish composer Jean Sibelius)

"Blessed are you when men cast insults at you, and persecute you, and say all kinds of evil against you falsely, on account of Me. Rejoice, and be glad, for your reward in heaven is great, for so they persecuted the prophets who were before you." (Matthew 5:11-12)

"When we are reviled, we bless; when we are persecuted, we endure." (1 Corinthians 4:12)

"To sum up, let all be harmonious, sympathetic, brotherly, kind-hearted, and humble in spirit; not returning evil for evil, or insult for insult, but giving a blessing instead; for you were called for the very purpose that you might inherit a blessing." (1 Peter 3:8-9)

13

Balancing Short-Term and Long-Term

Short-term and long-term are extremes that, as a pair, exist in robust tension: in Scripture, the earthly vs. the eternal. One enhances the significance of the other. Whenever separated, either one can become a trap that encourages dysfunctional behavior.

Short-Term Focus
1. Living for the Moment

And when Jacob had cooked stew, Esau came in from the field and he was famished; and Esau said to Jacob, "Please let me have a swallow of that red stuff there, for I am famished." Therefore his name was called Edom. But Jacob said, "First sell me your birthright." And Esau said, "Behold, I am about to die; so of what use then is the birthright to me?" And Jacob said, "First swear to me"; so he swore to him, and sold his birthright to Jacob. Then Jacob gave Esau bread and lentil stew; and he ate and drank, and rose and went on his way. Thus Esau despised his birthright. (Genesis 25:29–34)

So I commended pleasure, for there is nothing good for a man under the sun except to eat and to drink and to be merry. (Ecclesiastes 8:15)

2. Tyranny of the Urgent

Now as they were traveling along, [Jesus] entered a certain village; and a woman named Martha welcomed Him into her home. And she had a sister called Mary, who moreover was listening to the Lord's word, seated at His feet. But Martha was distracted with all her preparations; and she came up to Him, and said, "Lord, do You not care that my sister has left me to do all the serving alone? Then tell her to help me." But the Lord answered and said to her, "Martha, Martha, you are worried and bothered about so many things; but only a few things are necessary, really only one, for Mary has chosen the good part, which shall not be taken away from her." (Luke 10:38–42)

Long-Term Focus

1. Borrowing Trouble

Therefore do not be anxious for tomorrow; for tomorrow will care for itself. Each day has enough trouble of its own. (Matthew 6:34)

2. Too Much Curiosity

And so when they had come together, they were asking Him, saying, "Lord, is it at this time You are restoring the kingdom of Israel?" He said to them, "It is not for you to know times or epochs which the Father has fixed by His own authority; but you shall receive power when the Holy Spirit has come upon you; and you shall be My witnesses both in Jerusalem, and in all Judea and Samaria, and even to the remotest part of the earth." (Acts 1:6–8)

While he suffered, Job struggled to see beyond the immediate (short-term). When he compared his condition to the well-being of the wicked around him, Job floundered more.

Look at me and be appalled, and lay your hand over your mouth. When I remember, I am dismayed, and shuddering seizes my flesh. Why do the wicked live, reach old age, and grow mighty in power? Their offspring are established in their presence, and their descendants before their eyes. Their houses are safe from fear, and no rod of God is upon them. Their bull breeds without fail; their cow calves and does not miscarry. They send out their little boys like a flock, and their children dance. They sing to the tambourine and the lyre and rejoice to the sound of the pipe. They spend their days in prosperity, and in peace they go down to Sheol. (Job 21:5–13 ESV)

He could not see their end (long-term).

Why Do the Wicked Prosper?

"Why do the wicked prosper?" is a complaint as old as the Old Testament. It's a question that believers and pagans ask today; now a popular way to deny the existence of God.

During the Cycles of Dialogue, the fate of the wicked fascinated Job's friends. The topic appeared in each of their speeches, their attempt to understand Job's situation. Eliphaz, Bildad, and Zophar had relied upon their theology, the doctrine of divine ret-

ribution. It convinced them that Job was wicked because, according to their beliefs, the wicked always suffer. God judges them.

	ELIPHAZ	BILDAD	ZOPHAR
First Speech	Implicit	Implicit	Explicit
Second Speech	Explicit	Implicit	Implicit
Third Speech	Explicit	Implicit	None

Judgment: Job Is Wicked

The fate of the wicked was also a topic in six of Job's speeches
(chaps. 9–10, 12–14, 16–17, 21, 23–24, and 26–27). Citing his
own experiences (13:1–2), Job disagreed with the friends. Main-
taining his innocence motivated him too. Therefore, he insisted
that his suffering was not deserved punishment but mistreatment
by an unjust God who also allows the wicked to live carefree.

Job's third response to Bildad (chaps. 26-27) seems contradictory. It concludes with a graphic account of God punishing the
wicked (27:13-23). Why would Job criticize God as unjust throughout the Cycles of Dialogue, even in 27:2, but affirm Him as just
in 27:13-23? Because Job's closing remarks sound just like the
friends, some Old Testament scholars (e.g., Marvin Pope, H. H.
Rowley, and Norman Habel) seize 27:13-23 in order to create a
third speech for Zophar. The verses that precede 27:13-23, however, help to interpret it. Job chastised the friends in verses 7-12.
He called them "enemy" and "opponent" (27:7). Their folly warranted God's judgment which Job then describes in verses 13-23.
This eleven-verse section, therefore, should be read as critical of
the friends, not complimentary of God.

A Trick Question

The question "Why do the wicked prosper?" never appears verbatim in Scripture. Jeremiah 12:1 comes very close: "Why has the way of the wicked prospered? Why are all those who deal in treachery at ease?" Job 21:7 comes close too: "Why do the wicked live, reach old age, and grow mighty in power?" (ESV).

Asking and answering questions are routine behaviors for any educator. I welcome the raised hand. It means someone is awake, listening, and maybe interested! Who, what, when, and where don't worry me. Why and how, on the other hand, do. For example:

- How do we resolve the Middle East conflict?
- Why did the dinosaurs die?
- How does a person who never smoked get terminal lung cancer?
- Why didn't Gulf Coast prayers impede Hurricane Katrina?
- How do you know when it's right?

"Why do the wicked prosper?" is worse than difficult. It can't be answered as is. Not enough information has been given. The question lacks an adverb or adverbial phrase.

If, for instance, the adverb "eternally" is added, then "why do the wicked prosper?" can be answered easily. Do the wicked prosper eternally? No. Hell is their destiny (Luke 16:19–31).

If the adverbial phrase "on earth" is added, then "why do the wicked prosper?" can be answered easily. Do the wicked prosper on earth? Yes. They break the rules. They take unethical shortcuts. They use and abuse people. The wicked prosper because they are wicked. Our fallen world is vulnerable to the lawless despite its rules and regulations. The wicked also prosper in this life, albeit short-term, because God is merciful. He delays His judgment of their sin. Second Peter 3:9 explains, "The Lord is not slow about

His promise, as some count slowness, but is patient toward you, not wishing for any to perish but for all to come to repentance." God Himself has proclaimed, "I take no pleasure in the death of the wicked, but rather that the wicked turn from his way and live" (Ezekiel 33:11; see also 18:23, 32).

Jonah witnessed God's mercy lavished on Ninevites, but it displeased him. Filled with anger, the prophet whined, "O Lord, is not this what I said when I was yet in my country? That is why I made haste to flee to Tarshish; for I knew that you are a gracious God and merciful, slow to anger and abounding in steadfast love, and relenting from disaster" (Jonah 4:2 ESV).

The Long-Term Answer

Nearsightedness (myopia) and farsightedness (hyperopia) can be corrected with glasses, contacts, or surgery. Shortsightedness cannot. Presbyopia, a form of farsightedness, only affects older adults because the lens of one's eye loses elasticity over time. Conversely, shortsightedness occurs at any age, but curing it is cheaper. Among the treatment options, the spiritual one is best by far.

Paul prescribed, "Set your mind on the things above, not on the things that are on earth" (Colossians 3:2). Asking "How?" is a valid question. The apostle's answer can be found in his letters.

For we walk by faith, not by sight. (2 Corinthians 5:7)

For this reason I also suffer these things, but I am not ashamed; for I know whom I have believed and I am convinced that He is able to guard what I have entrusted to Him until that day. (2 Timothy 1:12)

Faith in God effectively elevates one's focus from the earthly to the eternal; applying the spiritual disciplines can stimulate one's faith.

In the classic *Celebration of Disciplines: The Path to Spiritual Growth*, Richard Foster profiled twelve practices.

Inward
Meditation
Prayer
Fasting
Study

Outward
Simplicity
Solitude
Submission
Service

Corporate
Confession
Worship
Guidance
Celebration

In 1991, NavPress published the book *Spiritual Disciplines for the Christian Life*. It profiles nine practices, three of which do not appear in Foster's book: namely, stewardship, evangelism, and journaling. Author Donald S. Whitney conceded, "This is by no means . . . an exhaustive list of the Disciplines of Christian living."

Foster clarified, "God has given us the Disciplines of the spiritual life as a means of receiving his grace. The Disciplines allow us to place ourselves before God so that he can transform us. . . . By themselves the Spiritual Disciplines can do nothing; they can only get us to the place where something can be done."[77]

Asaph, a psalmist, proved that the spiritual disciplines can salvage one's faith. He, like Job, had voiced frustration about how well the wicked lived (short-term). For him, it became a crisis of belief.

Surely God is good to Israel, to those who are pure in heart! But as for me, my feet came close to stumbling; my steps had almost slipped. For I was envious of the arrogant, as I saw the prosperity of the wicked. For there are no pains in their death; and their body is fat. They are not in trouble as other men; nor are they plagued like mankind. Therefore pride is their necklace; the garment of violence covers them. Their eye bulges from fatness; the imaginations of their heart run riot. They mock and wickedly speak of oppression. (Psalm 73:1–8)

The wicked disrespecting God unscathed (short-term) especially shocked him.

They have set their mouth against the heavens, and their tongue parades through the earth. . . . And they say, "How does God know? And is there knowledge with the Most High?" . . . Surely in vain I have kept my heart pure, and washed my hands in innocence. (vv. 9, 11, 13)

Before disillusionment could consume him, Asaph decided to worship yet again, consequently testifying, "I came into the sanctuary of God; then I perceived their end" (v. 17). A glimpse of the eternal recalibrated his perceptions of the present.

The Best Is Yet to Come

"This is it?" or "That's all?" is what disappointment sounds like. When Toto unmasked the Wizard, exposing him as a middle-aged Nebraskan, did your heart break for Dorothy and her travelling companions? What happened in Oz occurs every day on earth. The culprit is people, not just the wicked ones. Whether mean-spirited or well-intentioned, all people raise hopes too high and play favorites. Whether intentionally or unknowingly, all people trivialize, marginalize, and victimize.

"It is what it is," right? Actually, there's a whole lot more! Transcending "what is" requires faith, that which the empiricist dismisses, believing instead the physical senses. Trusting that a sovereign, loving God has secured what lies beyond the "here and now" requires faith, that which the secularist tragically cannot comprehend. "Faith means believing in advance what will only make sense in reverse."[78]

Thoughts to Ponder

"For I know that my Redeemer lives, and at the last he will stand upon the earth. And after my skin has been thus destroyed, yet in my flesh I shall see God, whom I shall see for myself, and my eyes shall behold, and not another. My heart faints within me!" (Job 19:25–27 ESV)

"For now we see in a mirror dimly, but then face to face; now I know in part, but then I shall know fully just as I also have been fully known." (1 Corinthians 13:12)

"Now faith is the substance of things hoped for, the evidence of things not seen." (Hebrews 11:1 KJV)

14

Appreciating and Applying Amazing Grace

A "rite of passage" is "a ritual performed in some cultures at times when an individual changes status (as from adolescence to adulthood)."[79] *Bar Mitzvah* and *Bath Mitzvah* divide childhood and adulthood for Jewish boys and girls, somewhat comparable to graduation and marriage in American culture. Age-specific rights (e.g., voting) or privileges (e.g., driving) also "separate the men from the boys."

Attitudes and behaviors, whether childish or mature, are less precise gauges: for example, when does one lose childhood innocence? Evidently, it can happen at any age because life is an unrelenting instructor. Its "pop quiz" might be physical abuse, serious illness, natural disaster, or divorcing parents; traumatic experiences that can cause a child to grow up very fast.

111

Have you spent substantive time with children? If so, you've heard their usual protest, "Not fair!" Innocence or naivety triggers the outcry. Parents and schoolteachers bear some of the blame because they create and perpetuate the illusion that life is fair, ensuring that (1) "Everyone gets a turn" (equal opportunity) and (2) "Everyone gets one" (same stuff, same amount). Sadly, not the real world!

Discovering that life isn't fair, therefore, is inevitable, the moment a chunk of childhood dies, when one loses childlike faith in all things being good. Noting that life wasn't fair, Job doubted that God was fair.

"Not Fair!"

During the Cycles of Dialogue, Job spoke frankly and unflatteringly about God.

> If it is a matter of power, behold, He is the strong one! And if it is a matter of justice, who can summon Him? Though I am righteous, my mouth will condemn me; though I am guiltless, He will declare me guilty. I am guiltless; I do not take notice of myself; I despise my life. It is all one; therefore I say, "He destroys the guiltless and the wicked." If the scourge kills suddenly, He mocks the despair of the innocent. The earth is given into the hand of the wicked; He covers the faces of its judges. If it is not He, then who is it? (Job 9:19–24)

> Although you know I am not guilty, no one can rescue me from your power. (10:7 NLT)

> I have become a laughingstock to my friends, though I called on God and he answered—a mere laughingstock, though righteous and blameless! Those who are at ease have contempt for misfortune as the fate of those whose

feet are slipping. The tents of marauders are undisturbed, and those who provoke God are secure—those God has in his hand. But ask the animals, and they will teach you, or the birds in the sky, and they will tell you; or speak to the earth, and it will teach you; or let the fish in the sea inform you. Which of all these does not know that the hand of the Lord has done this? (12:4–9 NIV)

Know then that God has wronged me, and has closed His net around me. Behold, I cry, "Violence!" but I get no answer; I shout for help, but there is no justice. (19:6–7)

Can anyone teach God knowledge, in that He judges those on high? One dies in his full strength, being wholly at ease and satisfied; his sides are filled out with fat, and the marrow of his bones is moist, while another dies with a bitter soul, never even tasting anything good. Together they lie down in the dust, and worms cover them. (21:22–26)

As God lives, who has taken away my right. (27:2)

Beware: Don't Compare!

Job had fallen into the "comparison" trap, a popular place to wallow, a deceptively dangerous place too. What soon incensed Job was not how much he had lost financially (net worth) but how his quality of life compared to the wicked that he saw firsthand (relative worth).

I will say to God, do not condemn me; let me know why you contend against me. Does it seem good to you to oppress, to despise the work of your hands and favor the designs of the wicked? (10:2–3 ESV)

The wicked had prospered as much when Job was rich. Hence, one may wonder, "Why now, Job? Why wasn't the problem of evil a problem for you beforehand?" The answer, in part, appears at the beginning of Eliphaz's first speech: "But now it has come to you, and you are impatient; it touches you, and you are dismayed" (4:5). Until "it" hits, whatever the hardship might be, our default is to be oblivious. Hear *my* confession: I noticed with envy every tightknit family *after* my parents divorced; I spotted the students struggling with a mental disorder, sitting in my class, *after* my daughter exhibited both depression and mania.

God Is More than Fair

Job's beef with God seemed legitimate, but he failed to recognize his bias. Considering himself righteous, Job demanded the justice that he merited (13:3, 18–19; 23:2–7; 31:35–37). No sinner realistically would prefer justice over mercy and grace. Observing the wicked, Job fumed that they received more mercy and grace than they deserved, but he overlooked the mercy and grace that he had received.

Matthew recorded a pertinent parable that no other Gospel writer did, "The Laborers in the Vineyard" (20:1–16). As controversial as it is, one might think that omitting the teaching would have been better!

The story is a kingdom parable. It focuses on the dealings between a landowner and five groups of laborers. The expectation of justice and the benefits of grace collide.

- The first group worked from "early in the morning" (20:1) to "evening" (v. 8).
- The second group worked nine hours (vv. 3–4).
- The third group worked six hours (v. 5).
- The fourth group worked three hours (v. 5).
- The fifth group worked one hour (vv. 6–7, 9).

Everyone received one denarius; unequal work for equal pay. Not fair!

By comparing themselves to the last group hired, the first group transformed quickly from working hard all day to being disgruntled at payday. Doing their best, making a difference, and pleasing the "boss" no longer satisfied them. Relationships at the workplace didn't matter. They could not see their employment as the landowner's grace.

Jesus's parable dramatizes how God relishes being gracious. Hence, He is better than fair because grace, by definition, is undeserved. Manifestations of His grace are "every good thing bestowed and every perfect gift" (James 1:17), the ultimate one being salvation which, according to Paul, is "eternal life in Christ Jesus our Lord" (Romans 6:23).

What is ironic is that recipients of God's grace try to regulate His graciousness. Jonah wanted to exclude Nineveh. The Pharisees grumbled that Jesus received sinners and ate with them (Luke 15:1–2). The leadership of the Jerusalem church initially opposed Peter's interaction with Gentiles (Acts 11:1–18).

Of course, no one can control God. He told Moses, "I will be gracious to whom I will be gracious, and will show compassion on whom I show compassion" (Exodus 33:19). Consequently, to resist His ministry of grace is to be the older brother and miss the party, standing outside yet looking in (Luke 15:25–32).

More than Fair: Our Standard of Living

The phrase "eye for eye, tooth for tooth" is a blunt way to describe fairness; namely, getting what one deserves. The Lord who is more than fair, however, commands His followers to heed a standard of living that exceeds quid pro quo. Jesus introduced the standard in the "Sermon on the Mount."

Forgiveness

Do not resist him who is evil; but whoever slaps you on your right cheek, turn to him the other also. (Matthew 5:39)

Generosity

And if anyone wants to sue you, and take your shirt, let him have your coat also. . . . Give to him who asks of you, and do not turn away from him who wants to borrow from you. (vv. 40, 42)

Service

And whoever shall force you to go one mile, go with him two. (v. 41)

Love

Love your enemies, and pray for those who persecute you. (v. 44)

None of these values can be quantified. On the contrary, love "doesn't keep score of the sins of others" (1 Corinthians 13:5 MSG). It "covers a multitude of sins" (1 Peter 4:8). When Peter tried to calculate forgiveness, Jesus halted him.

> Lord, how often shall my brother sin against me and I forgive him? Up to seven times? Jesus said to him, "I do not say to you, up to seven times, but up to seventy times seven." (Matthew 18:21–22)

Each of these values prods us to do more than the minimum which, in Jesus's day, the vile Gentiles embodied (5:47; 20:25). Whenever we live beyond what is fair, our "righteousness surpasses that of the scribes and Pharisees" (5:20) and we finally approximate the Father, being perfect as He is perfect (v. 48).

Thoughts to Ponder

"The grace of God is on the loose. Contrary to our expectations, counter to our assumptions, frustrating our judicial sentiments, and mocking our craving for control, the grace of God is turning the world upside down. God is shamelessly pouring out his lavish favor on undeserving sinners of all stripes and thoroughly stripping away our self-sufficiency."[80] (David Mathis)

"Let us therefore draw near with confidence to the throne of grace, that we may receive mercy and may find grace to help in time of need." (Hebrews 4:16)

"For judgment will be merciless to one who has shown no mercy; mercy triumphs over judgment." (James 2:13)

"Give, and it will be given to you; good measure, pressed down, shaken together, running over, they will pour into your lap. For by your standard of measure it will be measured to you in return." (Luke 6:38)

15

Acquiring Wisdom

nglish, unlike Akkadian or Latin, is a "living" language, meaning that it is still spoken. Its vocabulary changes constantly due to words being added or becoming archaic. A real time word count, therefore, cannot be determined. Consider:

- The Second Edition of the 20-volume *Oxford English Dictionary*, published in 1989, contains full entries for 171,476 words in current use, and 47,156 obsolete words. To this may be added around 9,500 derivative words included as subentries.[81]

- *Webster's Third New International Dictionary*, Unabridged, together with its 1993 Addenda Section, includes some 470,000 entries.[82]

English, like other languages living or extinct, has synonyms—"one of two or more words or expressions of the same language that have the same or nearly the same meaning in some or all senses."[83] The synonym is an antidote for monotonous writing. A caveat is that the use of synonyms can obscure shades of meaning. Consider part of the entry for "love" from my frayed 1977 edition of *The New American Roget's College Thesaurus in Dictionary Form*:

> **love**, fondness, liking; inclination, desire; regard, admiration, affection, tenderness, heart, attachment, yearning; gallantry; passion, flame, devotion, infatuation, adoration, idolatry.[84]

While "love" may be related more or less to the other words, it is uniquely superior.

What can be said about "love" can be said about "wisdom," too. English-speakers use "intelligence," "knowledge," "understanding," and "wisdom" interchangeably and unfortunately indiscriminately. As a result, the nuances of each word have faded. "Intelligence" is a capacity to know and to understand. "Knowledge" accumulates facts whereas "understanding" appreciates their significance. "Wisdom" applies both knowledge and understanding. It is know-how. The Hebrew noun, translated "wisdom," can signify skill (Exodus 28:3) or craftsmanship (31:3, 6).[85]

Where Can Wisdom Be Found?

Job 28 has been dubbed the "Wisdom Poem." It is poetry. The noun "wisdom" occurs four times in the chapter, compared to fifteen times in the rest of the book.

The Wisdom Poem consists of two parts, verses 1–11 and 12–28. The first eleven verses defy Job and his friends by profiling humans at their best, subduing creation (Genesis 1:28). Their feats mirror God's feats.

GOD	HUMANS
He reveals mysteries from the darkness, and brings the deep darkness into light. (12:22)	Man puts an end to darkness, and to the farthest limit he searches out the rock in gloom and deep shadow. (28:3) What is hidden he brings out to the light. (28:11b)
It is God who removes the mountains, they know not how, when He overturns them in His anger. (9:5)	He puts his hand on the flint; he overturns the mountains at the base. (28:9)
Who has cleft a channel for the flood? (38:25a)	He hews out channels through the rocks. (28:10a)

Content of the Wisdom Poem: Tribute to Human Achievement

Starting in verse 12 of the Wisdom Poem, the profile goes south. The remainder of the chapter exposes the glaring shortfall of human ingenuity. Mankind can excavate gems and extract precious metals but cannot obtain wisdom.

Where can wisdom be found? And where is the place of understanding? Man does not know its value, nor is it found in the land of the living. (vv. 12–13)

The questions that occur in verse 12 recur in verse 20. The Wisdom Poem answers them both implicitly and explicitly.

Implicitly

We, the readers, will not find wisdom in any speech by Job or his friends (chaps. 4–27).

Explicitly

God understands [wisdom's] way; and He knows its place. . . . Behold, the fear of the Lord, that is wisdom; and to depart from evil is understanding. (vv. 23, 28)

The Fear of the Lord

"Fear of the Lord" is a theme that links Job to Proverbs and Ecclesiastes.

The fear of the Lord is the beginning of knowledge. (Proverbs 1:7; see also 2:5 and 9:10)

The conclusion, when all has been heard, is: fear God and keep His commandments, because this applies to every person. (Ecclesiastes 12:13)

It is the "motto" of Old Testament wisdom literature.[86] James L. Crenshaw noted, "In some circles of the wise, the fear of Yahweh functioned as the compass point from which they took moral readings."[87]

The Hebrew noun, translated "fear," means awe or reverence when God is the focus.[88] Traditionally, scholars have identified it as the sage's synonym for "religion." This fear isn't, as von Rad rightly asserted, "something emotional."[89] It is a humble posture that thwarts arrogance, promoting teachability. Consequently, it leads to knowledge, understanding, and wisdom. "The 'fear' of God deals fundamentally with the heart and center of character, namely the position of the person *in relation* to God."[90]

Job was fearing God before (Job 1:1) and during two rounds of testing, a fact that God Himself reiterated (1:8; 2:3). Job also fell and worshiped (1:21). Elsewhere in the Old Testament, the verbs *napal* ("to fall") and *shacha* ("to worship") appear together ten times, either to respect a person (Ruth 2:10; 1 Samuel 20:41; 25:23; 2 Samuel 1:2; 9:6; 14:4, 22; 2 Kings 4:37) or to revere God (Joshua 5:14; 2 Chronicles 20:18).

In Job 1:1, 8 and 2:3, the Hebrew verb is a participle, denoting continuous action.

Following the tragedies, however, Job challenged God.

I loathe my life; I will give free utterance to my complaint; I will speak in the bitterness of my soul. I will say to God, do not condemn me; let me know why you contend against me. Does it seem good to you to oppress, to despise the work of your hands?" (10:1–3 ESV)

But I desire to speak to the Almighty and to argue my case with God. . . . Keep silent and let me speak; then let come to me what may. . . . Though he slay me, yet will I hope in him; I will surely defend my ways to his face. . . . Listen carefully to what I say; let my words ring in your ears. Now that I have prepared my case, I know I will be vindicated. Can anyone bring charges against me? If so, I will be silent and die. . . . Withdraw your hand far from me, and stop frightening me with your terrors. Then summon me and I will answer, or let me speak, and you reply to me. (13:3, 13, 15, 17–19, 21–22 NIV)

Oh, that I knew where I might find him, that I might come even to his seat! I would lay my case before him and fill my mouth with arguments. I would know what he would answer me and understand what he would say to me. (23:3–5 ESV)

Far be it from me that I should declare you right. (27:5)

I would declare to Him the number of my steps; like a prince I would approach Him. (31:37)

In order to reclaim Job, God confronted him from the whirlwind. It was a lengthy speech (38:1–39:30). Question after question targeted Job's insolence and pride to render him teachable again, but his reply was curt: "I lay my hand on my mouth. Once I have spoken, and I will not answer; even twice, and I will add no more" (40:4–5). Consequently, God spoke a second time (40:6–41:34). More questions!

Making Wisdom Available

In recent years, mentoring has become a buzz word. Titus 2:1–8 is a go-to text for pastors. Senior adults have been singled out, hearing the compelling challenge to share their wealth of wisdom, to take none of it to the grave.

God is not hesitant to share His wisdom. If His followers are unwilling to receive it, He will humble them (Proverbs 8:13; 15:33; 22:4; 28:14). He humbled Job.

Thoughts to Ponder

"Do not fear those who kill the body but are unable to kill the soul; but rather fear Him who is able to destroy both soul and body in hell." (Matthew 10:28)

"Do not be wise in your own eyes; fear the Lord and turn away from evil." (Proverbs 3:7)

"The fear of the Lord is the beginning of wisdom; all those who practice it have a good understanding. His praise endures forever!" (Psalm 111:10 ESV)

"Let the name of God be blessed forever and ever, for wisdom and power belong to Him." (Daniel 2:20)

"But if any of you lacks wisdom, let him ask of God, who gives to all men generously and without reproach, and it will be given to him." (James 1:5)

16

Rethinking Trials and Tragedies

After a greeting (James 1:1), James begins his letter with a command: "Consider it all joy, my brethren, when you encounter various trials, knowing that the testing of your faith produces endurance" (vv. 2–3). Three kinds of tests occur: (1) scheduled, (2) surprise (pop quiz), and (3) secret. A secret one yields the most realistic results because the person evaluated, being unaware, acts normally. Genesis 22 records the *secret* testing of Abraham.

In my twenty-four years as a professor, I have relied upon scheduled and surprise tests. My students have yet to rejoice. They don't realize how challenging it is to assess learning. The options that qualify as easy to administer and fair to take aren't many. Moreover, one size does not fit all. Students hate tests until they learn that the alternatives are a class presentation, term paper, or oral exam.

The testing that James mentions is one of life's surprises; suffering (see James 1:12; 4:10–12), no matter the form, shocks whomever it afflicts. Accordingly, Peter encouraged his readers:

Beloved, do not be surprised at the fiery trial when it comes upon you to test you, as though something strange were happening to you. But rejoice insofar as you share Christ's sufferings, that you may also rejoice and be glad when his glory is revealed. (1 Peter 4:12–13 ESV)

Peter himself received advanced notice of a test that Satan had scheduled. Jesus informed him, "Simon, Simon, behold, Satan has demanded permission to sift you like wheat; but I have prayed for you, that your faith may not fail" (Luke 22:31–32). Job had no forewarning, which is why he complained, "When I expected good, then evil came; when I waited for light, then darkness came" (Job 30:26).

"Results, Please!"

Whether scheduled, surprise, or secret, a test stands or falls by the kind of results that it generates. Analysts use two criteria to judge tests: validity and reliability. Does the test actually measure what it intends (validity)? Can the results be replicated (reliability)? If it can, then the test is accurate.[91]

According to James, testing by suffering produces endurance, a respectable result, a valuable character trait. *Hupomone*, translated "endurance," literally means abiding or remaining under; to hold up while being weighed down. In James 5:11, the Greek noun appears again: "Behold, we count those blessed who endured. You have heard of the endurance of Job and have seen the outcome of the Lord's dealings, that the Lord is full of compassion and is merciful."

Two biblical books, besides the book of Job, refer to Job: Ezekiel and James.

Following the action from chapter 1 to chapter 42 of Job, we the readers know the long and winding road this patriarch traveled to develop endurance. Was the secret test beneficial? The story contains enough data to do an assessment.

Was the test easy to administer?

Nothing is hard for God (Genesis 18:14). To test Job, He had deferred to the adversary. Nonetheless, after the first round of testing that ended with Job worshiping, God was annoyed. He told the adversary, "[Job] still holds fast his integrity, although you incited Me against him, to ruin him without cause" (Job 2:3). The Hebrew adverb translated "without cause" can be rendered "for nothing" (see 1:9).

Was the test fair to take?

A disadvantage of the secret test is that the subject may not have consented to be tested. Job *never* knew that his righteousness had been scrutinized. Moreover, his ten children and an unknown number of servants perished for the sake of the test unwittingly.

Was the test valid?

Doubting Job had prompted the test. The adversary asked,
Does Job fear God for no reason? Have
you not put a hedge around him and his
house and all that he has, on every side? You
have blessed the work of his hands, and his
possessions have increased in the land. But

> stretch out your hand and touch all that
> he has, and he will curse you to your face.
> (1:9–11 ESV)

God, therefore, permitted an examination of Job's motives. It confirmed God's pre-test appraisal: Job had been "blameless and upright . . . fearing God and turning away from evil" (1:8). Job would curse his birthday (chap. 3), but he never cursed God.

The test, although awful, inadvertently blessed Job. The adversary never intended to develop Job's perseverance (James 5:11) or deepen his intimacy with God. Job admitted afterwards, "I have heard of you by the hearing of the ear, but now my eye sees you" (Job 42:5 ESV).

Was the test reliable?

We will never know. The test's conditions cannot be replicated. Its notoriety prevents a secret sequel. To repeat the test, if it were possible, would be unconscionable because the first trial caused the loss of many lives (1:13–19).

Interpreting the Results

Our son Jonathan—better known as JP—earned a Master of Science in Medicine in order to be a physician assistant (PA). Four semesters of clinical rotations followed four semesters of arduous classes. Interacting with actual patients was both stressful and exhilarating. JP quickly learned how patients frustrate healthcare providers.

Patients know that they're ill, but they don't want to know why.

Proof: They refuse to be tested.

Patients know that they're ill, but they don't want to be well. *Proof:* They don't take their medications or make necessary lifestyle changes (diet or exercise; stop smoking or drinking).

Any test, medical or not, is a snapshot. It measures what is. What to do next is another decision.

Job's test was unique. It lasted significantly longer than an MRI or a catheterization. It ended when God restored Job (42:10–17). H. H. Rowley explained:

> In the Epilogue God's verdict is clearly expressed, and the discredited Satan has betaken himself from the scene. The trial is concluded when the verdict is given, and since the form of the trial was the sufferings of Job, those sufferings must cease. The Epilogue is demanded by the artistry of the book, and without it the work would be seriously incomplete. The restoration of Job's prosperity was not the reward of his piety, but the indication that the trial was over. Any judge who left a defendant to languish in prison after he had been declared innocent would be condemned as iniquitous, and if Job's trials had continued after he was acquitted it would have been similarly iniquitous.[92]

Job's test provided much more data because it "lingered." Initially, Job did well.

Prologue

Through all this Job did not sin nor did he blame God. (1:22)

In all this Job did not sin with his lips. (2:10)

Ultimately, Job did well.

Epilogue

And it came about after the Lord had spoken these words to Job, that the Lord said to Eliphaz the Temanite, "My anger burns against you and against your two friends, for you have not spoken of me what is right, as my servant Job has." (42:7 ESV)

For a while, however, Job languished. The test exposed the anger, pride, disrespect, and self-righteousness that lurked in his heart (Mark 7:20–23), moving God to confront and to correct; what any good teacher would do.

A Litmus Test

Cussing is just one of many bad habits. How does one know if the habit has been broken? Watch your favorite team lose to an underdog. Accidentally slam your hand in a door. Spill coffee on your shirt. Hit the brakes to avoid colliding with that driver who just cut in front of you. I do not know which is worse, the test or the results that it produces! Job proves that adversity is a very effective test; for tests of our character, the harder the better.

The fact that life's tests could be worse but are not is God's mercy. The fact that life's tests can be for our good is His grace.

Thoughts to Ponder

"When [God] has tried me, I shall come forth as gold." (Job 23:10; see also Proverbs 17:3)

"Search me, O God, and know my heart! Try me and know my thoughts! And see if there be any grievous way in me, and lead me in the everlasting way!" (Psalm 139:23-24 ESV; see also 26:2)

"You have been distressed by various trials, that the proof of your faith, being more precious than gold which is perishable, even though tested by fire, may be found to result in praise and glory and honor at the revelation of Jesus Christ." (1 Peter 1:6-7)

"If suffering is a megaphone, it is also a magnifying glass."[93] (Jill Briscoe)

"Job teaches us that the school of pain is the best teacher for those who want understanding."[94] (Glandion Carney and William Long)

17

Seeing Worth from God's Viewpoint

our-time NBA All-Star Latrell Sprewell played for the Golden State Warriors, New York Knicks, and Minnesota Timberwolves. He was paid $14.6 million during his last season (2004–2005) with the Timberwolves. Two days before that season started, Minnesota offered him a three-year, $21 million contract extension. Sprewell rejected it outright, claiming, "I'm at risk. I have a lot of risk here. I've got to feed my family."[95]

Sprewell got no sympathy. His outlandish objection did not endear himself to the rank and file like my wife who outnumber the rich and famous. Mary Ann and I have talked about the big money that professional athletes make. She's a teacher who likes sports but tackles the issue *as a teacher*. I'm a teacher who tackles the issue *as a sports fan*. Consequently, I repeat the rationalizations.

- An athlete is worth whatever a team is willing to pay.

- The higher-paid athletes attract more fans to the games, therefore generate more revenue for their teams, thus deserve their salaries.

Mary Ann remains unconvinced.

Self-Worth

In the English language, "self-esteem" (1657) and "self-worth" (1944) are not new words.[96] The concepts, albeit trendy, appear in the Bible.

You shall love your neighbor as yourself. (Leviticus 19:18)

Husbands ought also to love their own wives as their own bodies. He who loves his own wife loves himself; for no one ever hated his own flesh, but nourishes and cherishes it, just as Christ also does the church. (Ephesians 5:28–29)

The Bible never addresses low self-esteem, that which concerns the psychologist. Instead, biblical teaching wars against the inflated ego, better known as pride. Denying self, in fact, is a prerequisite to following Jesus (Luke 9:23).

To understand the biblical position requires acknowledging a bigger perspective: Is human worth relative or absolute? For an answer, Job is a suitable case study.

Relative or Absolute Worth?

The Prologue itemizes Job's "portfolio." It consisted exclusively of stocks, literally livestock: "His possessions also were 7,000 sheep, 3,000 camels, 500 yoke of oxen, [and] 500 female donkeys" (Job 1:3). His net worth earned the superlative, "That man was the greatest of all the men of the east" (v. 3).

In one afternoon, Job lost everything (vv. 13–22). What he actually lamented was a loss of respect. The community that had esteemed him no longer did.

[God] has made me a byword of the people, and I am one at whom men spit. (17:6)

God has made my brothers my enemies, and my friends have become strangers. My relatives have gone away, and my friends have forgotten me. My guests and my female servants treat me like a stranger; they look at me as if I were a foreigner. I call for my servant, but he does not answer, even when I beg him with my own mouth. My wife can't stand my breath, and my own family dislikes me. Even the little boys hate me and talk about me when I leave. All my close friends hate me; even those I love have turned against me. (19:13–19 NCV)

But now they mock me, men younger than I, whose fathers I would have disdained to put with my sheep dogs. Of what use was the strength of their hands to me, since their vigor had gone from them? Haggard from want and hunger, they roamed the parched land in desolate wastelands at night. In the brush they gathered salt herbs, and their food was the root of the broom bush. They were banished from human society, shouted at as if they were thieves. They were forced to live in the dry stream beds, among the rocks and in holes in the ground. They brayed among the bushes and huddled in the undergrowth. A base and nameless brood, they were driven out of the land. And now those young men mock me in song; I have become a byword among them. They detest me and keep their distance; they do not hesitate to spit in my face. Now that God has unstrung my bow and afflicted me, they throw off restraint in my presence. On my right the tribe attacks; they lay snares for my feet, they build their siege ramps against me. They break up my road; they succeed in destroying me. "No one can help him," they say. They advance as through a gaping breach; amid the ruins they come rolling in. Terrors overwhelm me; my dignity is driven away as by the wind, my safety vanishes like a cloud. (30:1–15 NIV; see also 29:2–12)

If net worth equals personal worth or if public opinion—somewhat influenced by net worth—determines one's value, then self-esteem would be more unstable than the stock market. Fortunately, it need not be; what Job learned during his encounter with God.

The first Yahweh Speech (38:1–40:2) showcased how the Creator manages the heavens and the earth; for instance, watering the desert (38:25–27) and positioning each constellation (vv. 31–33); feeding lions (vv. 39–40) and ravens (v. 41); admiring ostrich (39:13–18) and horses (vv. 19–25). Job had paid no attention to such details, but he did not miss the subtle point that they illustrated: if God cares greatly for lesser members of creation, how much greater will His care for Job be. Jesus, addressing His disciples, was more forthright.

Are not two sparrows sold for a penny? And not one of them will fall to the ground apart from your Father. But even the hairs of your head are all numbered. Fear not, therefore; you are of more value than many sparrows." (Matthew 10:29–31 ESV; see also 6:25–30; 12:11–12)

Net worth and public opinion do not matter to God. As Creator, He knows our value; His actions prove it.

Our Design

God used dust to create Adam (Genesis 2:7). The Hebrew noun *'apar* refers to loose earth.[97] Chemical analyses of the body, based upon the periodic table of elements, confirm how unremarkable our make-up is.[98] Hence, God transformed an ordinary mix of "ingredients" into a masterpiece. Ronald B. Allen commented, "Dust-man became living-man by God's grace; therein lies his humility and his dignity."[99]

> For you formed my inward parts; you knitted me together in my mother's womb. I praise you, for I am fearfully and wonderfully made. Wonderful are your works; my soul knows it very well. My frame was not hidden from you, when I was being made in secret, intricately woven in the depths of the earth. Your eyes saw my unformed substance; in your book were written, every one of them, the days that were formed for me, when as yet there was none of them. (Psalm 139:13–16 ESV)

> Your hands fashioned and made me, and now you have destroyed me altogether. Remember that you have made me like clay; and will you return me to the dust? Did you not pour me out like milk and curdle me like cheese? You clothed me with skin and flesh, and knit me together with bones and sinews. You have granted me life and steadfast love, and your care has preserved my spirit. (Job 10:8–12 ESV)

His Commitment and Care

How we treat something usually indicates its value, relative or absolute. We love what we cherish (Matthew 6:21; 13:44–46). Of course, to take what is valuable for granted happens too often;

undervaluing something or someone can manifest as neglect or abuse. Neither characterizes God.

> When I look at your heavens, the work of your fingers, the moon and the stars, which you have set in place, what is man that you are mindful of him, and the son of man that you care for him? Yet you have made him a little lower than the heavenly beings and crowned him with glory and honor. You have given him dominion over the works of your hands; you have put all things under his feet. (Psalm 8:3–6 ESV)

His Investment, Our Salvation

Paul reminded the church at Corinth, "For you know the grace of our Lord Jesus Christ, that though He was rich, yet for your sake He became poor, that you through His poverty might become rich" (2 Corinthians 8:9). To "redeem" (lit., buy back) us cost Him everything. The author of Hebrews, therefore, didn't exaggerate when he used the pronoun *telikoutos*, translated "so great," to modify salvation (Hebrews 2:3). Paul built on this when he said, "He who did not spare His own Son, but delivered Him up for us all, how will He not also with Him freely give us all things?" (Romans 8:32).

Beware of Inflation

Pride, according to Catholic theology, is one of the seven deadly sins. Despite the concerted efforts of priests and pastors to combat it, self is still a formidable foe.

In 2016, David Kinnaman and Gabe Lyons published their analysis of national public-opinion surveys by Barna Group. The book *Good Faith* divides into eighteen chapters. Chapter four, titled "The Tension We Feel and Why," focuses on a new moral code: the morality of self-fulfillment (see Table). What is so alarming is that adults in the United States and practicing Christians are more alike than different.[100]

THE NEW MORAL CODE *Morality of Self-Fulfillment*	% US Adults	% Practicing Christians
The best way to find yourself is by looking within yourself.	91	76
People should not criticize someone else's life choices.	89	76
To be fulfilled in life, you should pursue the things you desire most.	86	72
The highest goal of life is to enjoy it as much as possible.	84	66
People can believe whatever they want, as long as those beliefs don't affect society.	79	61
Any kind of sexual expression between two consenting adults is acceptable.	69	40

The New Moral Code

When self asserts its worth, it tends to inflate (see 1 Corinthians 8:1); the repulsive sounds of boasting are unfortunately familiar. Because self cannot control itself—self-control is a fruit of *the Spirit* (Galatians 5:22–23)—selfishness has been a global curse. Being selfish and devaluing others coincide. How sad!

Opting for God as the standard of our worth bypasses the quagmire of self-centeredness. His perspective permits us to see ourselves as we truly are. It is a needed dose of reality. His perspective also enables us to value the lives of others, not just our own, and to worship Him as worthy, what Job gladly did before God restored his net worth twofold (Job 42:1–6, 10–17).

Thoughts to Ponder

"Then God said, 'Let Us make man in Our image, according to Our likeness; and let them rule over the fish of the sea and over the birds of the sky and over the cattle and over all the earth, and over every creeping thing that creeps on the earth.' And God created man in His image, in the image of God He created him; male and female He created them." (Genesis 1:27-28)

"But we have this treasure in jars of clay, to show that the surpassing power belongs to God and not to us." (2 Corinthians 4:7 ESV)

"For we are His workmanship, created in Christ Jesus for good works, which God prepared beforehand, that we should walk in them." (Ephesians 2:10)

18

Not Forcing the Issue:
How Right Becomes Wrong

If it doesn't fit, cut it.
If it doesn't shut, slam it.
If it doesn't work, kick it.
If it doesn't behave, spank it.
If it doesn't close, sit on it.
If it doesn't understand, shout it.
If it doesn't respond, shake it or slap it.
If it doesn't leave, threaten it.
If it doesn't stack, trash it.
If it doesn't make sense, throw it against the wall.
If it doesn't move fast enough, give it a shove.

We love to be in control. If we're challenged, we'll resort to force, but might isn't always right. Case in point, forcing the issue.

The expression "forcing the issue" covers an array of acts, both effective and ineffective. Civil disobedience, for instance, can has-

ten the end of an injustice or the beginning of political independence. Mohandas K. Gandhi and Martin Luther King conducted
successful, nonviolent resistances; the demonstrators in Tian-
anmen Square (1989) did not. By crossing the Rubicon, Julius
Caesar caused the civil war that he won in order to be Ancient
Rome's supreme leader. By dumping tea from three British ships
into Boston Harbor, colonists started the split with Great Britain
four years before the Declaration of Independence.

"Forcing the issue" can be worse than ineffective. Japan, for
example, probably regretted bombing Pearl Harbor. Antiochus IV
tried to extinguish the Jewish religion by desecrating the Holy
of Holies (167 BCE). Instead, he sparked the Maccabean Revolt
which captured Jerusalem and rededicated the temple, a sweet victory that Hanukkah annually commemorates. Striking employees
can expedite workplace improvements, but American air traffic
controllers lost their jobs in 1981.

During the Cycles of Dialogue, Job understandably defended
himself. He was adamant. To prove how righteous he was, however, Job forced the issue, filing a lawsuit against God. His case
rested upon God being guilty. In the court of public opinion, he
pressured God to apologize; one of his tactics was flaunting his
own righteousness.

Righteousness vs. Self-Righteousness

The statement "The words of Job are ended" (Job 31:40) concludes his Second Monologue, a discourse that began in chapter 29 because the words of Eliphaz, Bildad, and Zophar finally
ended. Job's Second Monologue consists of three parts: "Before
the Tragedies" (chap. 29), "After the Tragedies" (chap. 30), and an
"Oath of Innocence" (chap. 31).

Part One (chap. 29) develops two themes: "The Good Old Days" (vv. 1–11, 21–25) and a "Résumé of Righteousness" (vv. 12–20). The résumé rivals the trial lawyer or social worker, the charity or government agency. It presents Job as *the* victim's advocate, intervening on behalf of the poor (v. 12), orphan (v. 12), dying (v. 13), widow (v. 13), blind (v. 15), lame (v. 15), needy (v. 16), and stranger (v. 16). It even pictures Job confronting victimizers (v. 17).

Job's self-promotion compares to two others that appear in the New Testament: a Pharisee (Luke 18:11–12) and Paul (2 Corinthians 11:16–33).

The Pharisee

The Pharisee stood by himself and prayed; "God, I thank you that I am not like other people—robbers, evildoers, adulterers—or even like this tax collector. I fast twice a week and give a tenth of all I get." (Luke 18:11–12 NIV)

Paul

Are they Hebrews? So am I. Are they Israelites? So am I. Are they descendants of Abraham? So am I. Are they servants of Christ? (I speak as if insane) I more so; in far more labors, in far more imprisonments, beaten times without number, often in danger of death. Five times I received from the Jews thirty-nine lashes. Three times I was beaten with rods, once I was stoned, three times I was shipwrecked, a night and a day I have spent in the deep. I have been on frequent journeys, in dangers from rivers, dangers from robbers, dangers from my countrymen, dangers from the Gentiles, dangers in the city, dangers in the wilderness, dangers on the sea, dangers among false brethren; I have been in labor and hardship, through many sleepless nights, in hunger and thirst, often without food, in cold and exposure. Apart from such external things, there is the daily pressure upon me of concern for all the churches. (2 Corinthians 11:22–28)

Unlike Paul, the Pharisee was a fictional character in one of Jesus's parables. Unlike the Pharisee or Job, Paul realized he was bragging (2 Corinthians 11:16–19).

Modern biblical scholarship—since the Age of Enlightenment (18th century)—has rejected Mosaic authorship of the Pentateuch. Among the reasons given, Moses could not have written Numbers 12:3; "Now the man Moses was very humble, more than any man who was on the face of the earth." The doubters legitimately ask, "Can one be proud about being humble and still be humble?"

"Can one trumpet being righteous and still be righteous?" is also a legitimate question. The answer, based upon the Sermon on the Mount (Matthew 6:1–18), is "No!" Three times (vv. 2, 5, 16), Jesus called that kind of individual a hypocrite, His preferred description of Pharisees. Jesus did concede that Pharisaic teaching was correct: "All that they tell you, do and observe" (23:3). He even charged His disciples, "Unless your righteousness surpasses that of the scribes and Pharisees, you shall not enter the kingdom of heaven" (5:20). Pride, however, tainted the righteousness of the Pharisees: "They do all their deeds to be noticed by men" (23:5).

Analysis of Self-Righteousness

To do what is right honors God and helps others. Self-righteousness, on the other hand, is self-serving: specifically, being righteous for the sake of recognition or being judgmental. For the self-righteous person, just doing what is right doesn't satisfy.

Motive matters in a criminal case; it matters to God, too. Hence, for Him, egocentric intent discredits righteous deeds, no matter how great they might be.

Because it is offensive, self-righteousness is easy to spot, apparent to everyone but the one at fault. On February 21, 1988, televangelist Jimmy Swaggart informed his Baton Rouge congregation, "I have sinned."[101] Local and national media relished reporting the details of his sexual misconduct. At the time, I was a graduate student at New Orleans Baptist Theological Seminary, just seventy-five miles southeast on Interstate 10. On our campus, Swaggart became the butt of jokes. Some classmates were gleeful that the famous preacher may have been exposed as a fraud. Our professor, Fisher Humphreys, did not aid and abet those points of view. Before lecturing, as had been his custom, he prayed, saying, "Father, forgive our brother's unrighteousness and forgive our self-righteousness."

Job was blind to his own self-righteousness until the second Yahweh Speech. Nothing in Scripture is like Job 40:9–14. Responding to attacks from Job, God invited the human to be God.

> Does an arm like God belong to you? With voice, can you thunder like him? Deck yourself, I pray, with glory and grandeur. Be clothed with splendor and majesty. Scatter the outbursts of your anger. Look at all the proud; then, humiliate each one. Look at all the proud; then, humble each one. Cast down the wicked beneath them. Hide the proud and the wicked together in the dust. Bind their faces in darkness. Then, even I will praise you, that your right hand can save you. (my translation)

To sit on heaven's throne requires more than rhetorical skills (v. 9) or the proper attire (v. 10). Issuing six commands in verses 11–12, God admonished Job to subdue pride. It is the greatest threat to sovereignty. God's challenge could have been blunter: "Job, whenever you tackle pride, first look in the mirror!"

What's Your Motive?

In the book *Classic Christianity*, Bob George wrote, "We have simply not come to grips with the fact that it isn't *hard* to live the Christian life. It's *impossible*! Only Christ can live it."[102] The reasons are legion: the "big three," according to Christian theology, are the world, the flesh, and the devil. Sinning is easy; moreover, "Bad company corrupts good morals" (1 Corinthians 15:33).

Jesus apprised His followers, "Do not let your left hand know what your right hand is doing" (Matthew 6:3). That instruction really reveals why the Christian life is ~~hard~~ impossible. No standard is higher than God's; it obligates head, heart, and hand. Consequently, to do what is right isn't enough; our why is as important as the what.

Thoughts to Ponder

"These three men ceased answering Job, because he was righteous in his own eyes. But the anger of Elihu, the son of Barachel the Buzite, of the family of Ram burned; against Job his anger burned, because he justified himself before God." (Job 32:1-2)

"Thus says the Lord, 'Let not a wise man boast of his wisdom, and let not the mighty man boast of his might, let not a rich man boast of his riches; but let him who boasts boast of this, that he understands and knows Me, that I am the Lord who exercises lovingkindness, justice, and righteousness on earth; for I delight in these things,' declares the Lord." (Jeremiah 9:23-24)

"For it is not the one who commends himself who is approved, but the one whom the Lord commends." (2 Corinthians 10:18 ESV)

19

Approaching God on His Terms

I *love* a bargain; I *hate* to bargain. Meanwhile, my wife Mary Ann, the "Wheeler-Dealer," insists, "The price tag is not the final price. Negotiate!"

Salespersons sigh when Mary Ann walks out; they salivate when I show up. Hear my plight: a "bait-and-switch" victim, assaulted by hidden charges and unforeseen costs, without recourse. I get less than I bargain for.

Meanwhile, my wife has earned two degrees: a Bachelor of Science in math education and a Master of Science in mathematics. In her hand, a calculator is a weapon. She can compute amortization tables!

Mary Ann does not hesitate to utter *her* ultimatum: "May I speak with someone who cares whether or not you have my business?" Sweet deals usually follow.

- Extra add-ons, additional markdowns, and, of course, free delivery

- Expired coupons? *No* problem.

My wife is a successful real estate agent. No surprise. Nobody intimidates her; I certainly don't. She realizes that the worst outcome of any haggling is a "no" answer. She quotes James 4:2, "You have not because you ask not."

As skillful as Mary Ann is, she knows that a better "deal" could not be brokered than what God already offers: namely, grace. At first, Job would not have agreed with my wife.

Taking Matters into His Own Hands

After two rounds of tragedies, Job found himself in unfamiliar territory: destitute, diseased, and disrespected. The loss of respect hurt him the most. He deduced that God was both problem and solution, the reason for his predicament and the sole power to end that injustice.

Though Job desperately wanted to talk to God, to plead his case, the confrontation and conversation panicked him.

How shall a man be right with God? If he desired to contend with God, he could not answer him once out of a thousand times. (Job 9:2–3, my translation)

How then can I answer Him, and choose my words before Him? For though I were right, I could not answer; I would have to implore the mercy of my judge. If I called and He answered me, I could not believe that He was listening to my voice. . . . If it is a matter of power, behold, He is the strong one! And if it is a matter of justice, who can summon Him? Though I am righteous, my mouth will condemn me; though I am guiltless, He will declare me guilty. (9:14–16, 19–20)

Though [God] slay me, I will hope in him; yet I will argue my ways to his face. (13:15 ESV)

Today also my complaint is bitter; my hand is heavy on account of my groaning. Oh, that I knew where I might find him, that I might come even to his seat! I would lay my case before him and fill my mouth with arguments. I would know what he would answer me and understand what he would say to me. Would he contend with me in the greatness of his power? No, he would pay attention to me. There an upright man could argue with him, and I would be acquitted forever by my judge. . . . But he is unchangeable, and who can turn him back? What he desires, that he does. For he will complete what he appoints for me, and many such things are in his mind. Therefore I am terrified at his presence; when I consider, I am in dread of him. God has made my heart faint; the Almighty has terrified me; yet I am not silenced because of the darkness, nor because thick darkness covers my face. (23:2–7, 13–17 ESV)

Conventional wisdom today would have been passionate but advised Job poorly.

- Wear a power (i.e., red) tie.
- Look God in the eye.
- Breathe diaphragmatically.
- Never let Him see you sweat.
- Be confident but not arrogant.
- Be conversant but not talkative.
- Don't slouch.
- Don't chew gum.

In his third speech, Eliphaz offered Job the conventional wisdom of the Ancient Near East.

Submit to God and be at peace with him; in this way prosperity will come to you. Accept instruction from his mouth and lay up his words in your heart. If you return to the Almighty, you will be restored: if you remove wickedness far from your tent. (22:21–23 NIV)

Unfortunately, Eliphaz's counsel failed to persuade. Job opted to be carefree and cavalier.

> O that a hearing were given to me. Behold my mark— let the Almighty answer me. And the indictment which my adversary has written, surely I would carry it on my shoulder; I would bind it to myself like a crown. I would declare to Him the number of my steps; like a prince I would approach Him. (31:35–37)

Job's posturing may impress the timid, everyone who has dreamed about giving authority figures a piece of his or her mind, but it failed to break heaven's silence.

What a God!

The Old Testament records a few examples of correct etiquette in front of royalty. When Pharaoh summoned Joseph, he quickly shaved and changed clothes (Genesis 41:14). The cupbearer Nehemiah knew to be pleasant; thus, he tried to fake it (Nehemiah 2:1–2). Esther informed Mordecai, "All the king's servants and the people of the king's provinces know that for any man or woman who comes to the king to the inner court who is not summoned, he has but one law, that he be put to death, unless the king hold out to him the golden scepter so that he may live" (Esther 4:11).

If God is the King of kings (1 Timothy 6:15; Revelation 17:14; 19:16), how would He expect us to act in His presence? Bart Millard penned and sang the beloved refrain:

> *Surrounded by Your glory,*
> *What will my heart feel?*
> *Will I dance for You, Jesus,*

Or in awe of You be still?
Will I stand in Your presence
Or to my knees will I fall?
Will I sing hallelujah,
Will I be able to speak at all?
I can only imagine.
I can only imagine.[103]

The song by MercyMe anticipates seeing Jesus *in heaven*. Hebrews 4:16 instructs us how to approach the Lord God *now*: "Let us therefore draw near with confidence to the throne of grace, that we may receive mercy and may find grace to help in time of need." Indeed, "to Him who sits on the throne, and to the Lamb, be blessing and honor and glory and dominion forever and ever" (Revelation 5:13), but what distinguishes His throne—typically a seat of power and authority—is grace.

> Since therefore, brethren, we have confidence to enter the holy place by the blood of Jesus, by a new and living way which He inaugurated for us through the veil, that is, His flesh, and since we have a great priest over the house of God, let us draw near with a sincere heart in full assurance of faith, having our hearts sprinkled clean from an evil conscience and our bodies washed with pure water. (Hebrews 10:19–22; see also 4:14–15)

If this sounds too good to be true, read the "Parable of the Prodigal Son" (Luke 15:11–32) again. Jesus showed us God the Father through a Jewish father who had two troubled sons.

The younger son demanded his inheritance and independence. In a far country, he wasted no time to waste what his father had worked years to amass. "Prodigal" means "characterized by wasteful expenditure."[104]

Hungry and humiliated, surrounded by swine, the younger son "came to his senses" (v. 17). He had hit bottom. Contemplating how to go home, he memorized a proposal, "Father, I have sinned against heaven, and in your sight; I am no longer worthy to be called your son; make me as one of your hired men" (vv. 18–19, 21).

The father ignored what likely had been an Oscar-worthy performance. As head of the household, he could. He owed this son nothing, which is why reinstating him seemed scandalous to the older son.

Certainly, Jesus's parable targets Pharisees who had grumbled, "This man receives sinners and eats with them" (vv. 2–3). The older son personifies the Pharisees; the reason that the story does not end well (vv. 25–32). Nevertheless, the story also shows how we all underestimate God the Father. The younger son never knew his father had hoped for his return day after day. He concluded his father couldn't love him anymore. He didn't expect his father to offer a better deal than the hourly wages of a laborer. A gift of grace foiled this rebel's poor attempt to return on his own terms.

The prodigal would have settled for second class, demoted to servant rather than restored as son. In contrast, Job demanded his "old job" back, but his tactics were unsuccessful. He couldn't intimidate God with legal action or impress Him by touting his righteous past. What Job wanted (exoneration) was less than what he got (more unconditional love) when God revealed Himself freely from the whirlwind. How many can recount a one-on-one encounter on earth with the Creator, being in a place that His presence hallowed and hearing personal words audibly?

I want to scale the utmost height
And catch a gleam of glory bright;
But still I'll pray till heav'n I've found,
"Lord, lead me on to higher ground."

Lord, lift me up and let me stand,
By faith, on heaven's tableland,
A higher plane than I have found;
Lord, plant my feet on higher ground.[105]

Thoughts to Ponder

"Come to Me, all who are weary and heavy-laden, and I will give you rest. Take My yoke upon you, and learn from Me, for I am gentle and humble in heart; and you shall find rest for your souls. For My yoke is easy, and My load is light." (Matthew 11:28-30)

"Therefore having been justified by faith, we have peace with God through our Lord Jesus Christ, through whom also we have obtained our introduction by faith into this grace in which we stand; and we exult in hope of the glory of God." (Romans 5:1-2)

"The Spirit Himself bears witness with our spirit that we are children of God, and if children, heirs also, heirs of God and fellow heirs with Christ, if indeed we suffer with Him in order that we may also be glorified with Him." (Romans 8:16-17)

"See how great a love the Father has bestowed upon us, that we should be called children of God; and such we are. For this reason the world does not know us, because it did not know Him." (1 John 3:1)

20

Emulating Elihu

T he name Elihu means "He is my God." Readers of the book of Job might refer to him as Eli-Who. The Prologue introduces every character in the story except him. Nobody knows why, but Old Testament scholars have theories. Like Melchizedek, Elihu appears out of nowhere and disappears without a trace.

In the story, Elihu speaks more than any character other than Job. He spoke at length about God; in doing so, he spoke more than God!

Most Old Testament scholars have not been kind to Elihu. Four words summarize their assessment: impetuous, unoriginal, ineffectual, and interpolation. According to them, Elihu talked big (impetuous) but failed to deliver.

> I am young in years, and you are aged; therefore I was timid and afraid to declare my opinion to you. I said, "Let days speak, and many years teach wisdom." But it is the

spirit in man, the breath of the Almighty that makes him understand. It is not the old who are wise, nor the aged who understand what is right. Therefore I say, "Listen to me; let me also declare my opinion." Behold, I waited for your words, I listened for your wise sayings, while you searched out what to say. I gave you my attention, and, behold, there was none among you who refuted Job or who answered his words. (Job 32:6–12 ESV)

Pay attention, O Job, listen to me; keep silent and let me speak. Then if you have anything to say, answer me; speak, for I desire to justify you. If not, listen to me; keep silent, and I will teach you wisdom. (33:31–33)

Even though Elihu talked a lot, he did not add anything to the discussion (unoriginal). After he finally finished, no one responded positively or negatively (ineffectual). Since no hint of him exists before chapter 32 and deleting his speeches does no harm to the story, Elihu must have been inserted by someone else (interpolation) after the book had been completed.

Elihu: A Second Look

Procter & Gamble has successfully demonized dandruff. Commercials for its shampoo Head & Shoulders warned viewers years ago, "You never get a second chance to make a first impression."[106] If first impressions are consequential, then Elihu does hurt himself. From his first word, he comes across as brash and abrasive. His demand "Let me speak" clangs for seventeen verses (32:6–22). His statement "I will speak" lasts seven verses (33:1–7).

If one can sift through the bluster—really, passion—to observe his heart, then Elihu looks quite different. His unforeseen role enhances the intensifying conflict between Job and God. His words are stirring when compared to the speeches of Job and Job's friends.

Plot Analysis: Anticlimax

Job's Second Monologue concluded with a dare, the Oath of Innocence (chap. 31). Before the Oath ended, Job taunted God. It was a final jab.

> O that a hearing were given to me. Behold my mark— let the Almighty answer me. And the indictment which my adversary has written, surely I would carry it on my shoulder; I would bind it to myself like a crown. I would declare to Him the number of my steps; like a prince I would approach Him. (vv. 35–37)

The disrespect no doubt is disturbing. Readers need not be overly sensitive to wonder, "How will God respond? Surely, He will show up. Will Job then burn up? Could the statement 'The words of Job are ended' (v. 40) be prophetic?"

Because the suspense had never been greater, it convinced Northrop Frye to regard Job's Second Monologue as the climax of the book.[107] The unannounced arrival of Elihu, therefore, isn't just a surprise; it is an interruption, maybe a disruption.

If Elihu isn't an interpolation, then he does serve some purpose. Could he be "comic relief"?

> **comic relief** *n* (1875): a relief from the emotional tension of a drama that is provided by the interposition of a comic episode or element.[108]

A better proposal is the literary term "anticlimax." It denotes a specific moment when, after mounting tension, events turn unexpectedly; an undeniable letdown.[109]

Elihu has received a lukewarm reception, but the expression "right place, right time" befits him. From the instant that he enters the story, he delays the Yahweh Speeches, thus heightening their impact.

Job must have been disappointed to hear the voice of *another* human being, but Elihu's appearance spoke volumes. Job learned what sovereignty means. God cannot be coerced, ever. Job's drastic measures secured none of his demands: he had wanted Yahweh; he got Elihu!

Content Analysis: The Warm-up Act

Elihu may have been long-winded, but, unlike Job or Job's friends, he was a successful speaker. First, his speeches changed the subject for good. The fate of the wicked had been the focus of Job's friends: 99.5/203 verses. God—specifically His goodness, righteousness, and creative power—had been the focus of Job and Elihu, but Elihu praised what Job had doubted or criticized.

	GOD	JOB'S THREE FRIENDS
First Cycle		
1st Speech	6:4, 8–10, 14b; 7:7–21	6:14–30; 7:7–11
2nd Speech	9:2–24, 28–35; 10:2–22	none
3rd Speech	12:6, 9–10, 13–25; 13:3, 7–11, 15–16, 20–28; 14:1–6, 13–22	12:2–5, 7–12; 13:1–19
TOTAL	**121.5 Verses**	**51 Verses**
Second Cycle		
1st Speech	16:6–17, 20b–21; 17:3–4, 6	16:2–5, 20a; 17:4–5, 10
2nd Speech	19:5–22, 26–27	19:2–6, 14b, 21–22, 28–29
3rd Speech	21:9b, 17b, 19–20, 22	21:2–5, 27–34
TOTAL	**39.5 Verses**	**29 Verses**
Third Cycle		
1st Speech	23:2–17; 24:1–12, 21–25	none
2nd Speech	26:5–14; 27:2–3, 7–23	26:2–4; 27:2–6, 11–12
TOTAL	**62 Verses**	**10 Verses**

Focus of Job's Speeches in the Cycles of Dialogue

	God	Job	Friends	Wicked
1st Speech	32:8b, 22; 33:4, 6, 12–18, 26, 29–30	32:6–7, 10, 14; 33:1, 5–13, 31–33	32:6–7, 10–13, 14b–16	no mention
2nd Speech	34:10–15, 17–19, 21–33a	34:5, 16, 33–37	34:2–10, 16, 33–37	34:22, 26
3rd Speech	35:2b, 6–7, 10–15	35:2–8, 14, 16	35:4b–5	35:12
4th Speech	36:2–13, 15–16, 22–33; 37:2–7, 10–15, 18–24	36:2, 4, 16–21, 24; 37:14–19	no mention	36:6a, 13–14, 17
TOTAL	89.5 Verses	48 Verses	25 Verses	6.5 Verses

Focus of Elihu's Speeches

	His Goodness	His Righteousness	His Creative Power
1st Speech	33:23–30	no mention	33:4, 6
2nd Speech	34:13–15	34:10–12, 21–30	34:19b
3rd Speech	35:10b–11	35:2, 5–8, 12–15	35:10a
4th Speech	36:15–16, 31b	36:3, 5a, 6–16, 23b, 31a; 37:23b	36:24–25, 27–33; 37:2–18
TOTAL	15 Verses	36 Verses	29 Verses

Content of Elihu's Speeches: God

Second, Yahweh came after Elihu spoke. The memorized theology of Job's friends did not prod God. Job's antics certainly didn't. Only Elihu was God's herald: whetting appetites with a foretaste of the divine; preparing hearts for worship.

A Role Model

In 1991, Quaker Oats contracted Michael Jordan to promote its product, Gatorade. An ad campaign featured the jingle and slogan "Be Like Mike." Gatorade sales failed to rise, but the commercial inspired smiles, sing-a-longs, and at least two sequels.[110]

Gatorade marketers haven't seen my jump shot. I'm a lefty. If I became a "gym rat," I still couldn't be like Mike, but don't shed a tear for me. I have a different aspiration. I want to be like Elihu, ready to talk about my God and capable of turning an ordinary conversation into spiritual contemplation. I want to be like Elihu. God was his first love. Elihu knew Him well enough to keep on talking. I want to be like Elihu. May others sense God rather than notice me. After his last speech, Elihu abruptly exited center stage. He didn't want to interrupt God.

Thoughts to Ponder

"And Elihu continued, and said: 'Bear with me a little, and I will show you, for I have yet something to say on God's behalf. I will get my knowledge from afar and ascribe righteousness to my Maker. For truly my words are not false; one who is perfect in knowledge is with you. Behold, God is mighty, and does not despise any; he is mighty in strength of understanding.'" (Job 36:1-5 ESV)

"He must increase, but I must decrease." (John 3:30)

"When I came to you, I did not come with eloquence or human wisdom as I proclaimed to you the testimony about God. For I resolved to know nothing while I was with you except Jesus Christ and him crucified." (1 Corinthians 2:1-2 NIV)

21

Celebrating God Is Free

On October 27, 1967, my parents and I immigrated to the United States. We landed at LaGuardia Airport, but our destination was Toledo, Ohio. We came for economic opportunity. Until I became an adult, I did not fathom how much my parents had sacrificed for a better life.

Immigrants journey to America for a host of reasons, foremost among them is freedom. At America's "front door," millions knocked, processed at Ellis Island. They had been beckoned by a statue. Emma Lazarus composed the famous words mounted upon Lady Liberty's pedestal.

> *Not like the brazen giant of Greek fame,*
> *With conquering limbs astride from land to land;*
> *Here at our sea-washed, sunset gates shall stand*
> *A mighty woman with a torch, whose flame*
> *Is the imprisoned lightning, and her name*

Mother of Exiles. From her beacon-hand
Glows world-wide welcome; her mild eyes command
That air-bridged harbor that twin cities frame.
"Keep, ancient lands, your storied pomp!" cries she
With silent lips. "Give me your tired, your poor,
Your huddled masses yearning to breathe free,
The wretched refuse of your teeming shore.
Send these, the homeless, tempest-tost to me,
I lift my lamp beside the golden door!"[111]

The Pilgrims were the New World's first freedom-seekers. They had been persecuted by the Church of England. Their willingness to pay such a steep price to be free was not a historical exception. On March 20, 1775, Virginia delegate Patrick Henry echoed the Pilgrims' spirit: "Is life so dear, or peace so sweet, as to be purchased at the price of chains and slavery? Forbid it, Almighty God! I know not what course others may take; but as for me, give me liberty or give me death!"[112] In 1945, New Hampshire actually adopted the motto "Live free or die."[113]

What does it mean "to be free"? Life situation determines how a person might answer: to be free *from* adversity (e.g., leaving an abusive relationship) or to be free *for* opportunity (e.g., trading rent for a mortgage).

To Be Free From
- Confinement (Prisoner)
- Tyranny (Asylum Seeker)
- Debt (Borrower)
- Pain (Patient)
- Authority (Teenager)

To Be Free For
- Career (College Graduate)
- Retirement (Senior Adult)

In the book of Job, God taught Job how free He was.

God Is Free: The Details

During the Cycles of Dialogue, Job and his friends agreed sometimes. They all believed that God is omnipotent and omniscient.

Speaker: Job

Wisdom and might are with God. Counsel and understanding belong to Him. Behold, He tears down and it will not be rebuilt. He imprisons a man and he will not be loosed. Behold, He restrains the waters and they will dry up. He sends them and they will devastate the land. Strength and sound wisdom are with God. The mistaken and the misleader belong to Him. He leads counselors away barefoot. He makes fools out of judges. He loosens the bond of kings but girds their loins with a waistcloth. He leads priests away barefoot. He overturns the settled. He takes away the speech of the trustworthy and the discernment of elders. He pours out contempt upon nobles. He weakens the strong. He uncovers the unsearchable things from darkness. He brings deep shadows out to the light. He makes the nations great, then destroys them. He expands the nations, then leads them away. He takes away the mind of the chiefs over the people of the land, then makes them wander in trackless waste. Without light, they grope in darkness. He causes them to wander like the drunkard. (Job 12:13–25, my translation)

Speaker: Eliphaz

But if I were you, I would appeal to God; I would lay my cause before him. He performs wonders that cannot be fathomed, miracles that cannot be counted. He provides rain for the earth; he sends water on the countryside. The lowly he sets on high, and those who mourn are lifted to safety. He thwarts the plans of the crafty, so that their hands achieve no success. He catches the wise in their craftiness, and the schemes of the wily are swept away. Darkness comes upon them in the daytime; at noon they grope as in the night. He saves the needy from the sword in their mouth; he saves them from the clutches of the powerful. So the poor have hope, and injustice shut its mouth. (5:8–16 NIV)

Speaker: Bildad

Dominion and awe belong to Him who establishes peace in His heights. Is there any number to His troops? And upon whom does His light not rise? (25:2–3)

Speaker: Zophar

Can you discover the depths of God? Can you discover the limits of the Almighty? They are high as the heavens, what can you do? Deeper than Sheol, what can you know? Its measure is longer than the earth, and broader than the sea. If He passes by or shuts up, or calls an assembly, who can restrain Him? (11:7–10)

The prefix "omni," a form of the Latin noun *omnis*, means "all." To be all-powerful (omnipotence) and all-knowing (omniscience) is, for us, inconceivable. As a result, we *always* underestimate God (Ephesians 3:20).

Job seemed to understand that "limitless" or "unrestricted" describes God.

> He performs wonders that cannot be fathomed, miracles that cannot be counted. When he passes me, I cannot see him; when he goes by, I cannot perceive him. If he snatches away, who can stop him? Who can say to him, "What are you doing?" (9:10–12 NIV)

> But he is unchangeable, and who can turn him back? What he desires, that he does. (23:13 ESV)

Job's actions, however, contradicted his words. Why did he think that a lawsuit could intimidate an eternal Being that length, width, and height do not define? Why did he expect that his Oath of Innocence (chap. 31) could outsmart the very One who "searches all hearts, and understands every intent of the thoughts" (1 Chronicles 28:9)?

God didn't show up "on time" when Job demanded. When He did arrive, He didn't say what Job had wanted to hear. The Second Yahweh Speech paraded two monsters, Behemoth and Leviathan. Behemoth appears nowhere else in Scripture, but Leviathan does.

> Let those curse [the day on which I was born] who curse the day, who are prepared to rouse Leviathan. (Job 3:8; speaker, Job)

> You crushed the heads of Leviathan; you gave him as food for the creatures of the wilderness. (Psalm 74:14 ESV)

> There the ships go to and fro, and Leviathan, which you formed to frolic there. (Psalm 104:26 NIV)

> In that day the Lord will take his terrible, swift sword and punish Leviathan the swiftly moving serpent, the coil-

ing, writhing serpent, the dragon of the sea. (Isaiah 27:1 NLT)

Later Jewish literature adds to the mystique of these creatures.

Then thou didst keep in existence two living creatures; the name of one thou didst call Behemoth and the name of the other Leviathan. And thou didst separate one from the other, for the seventh part where the water had been gathered together could not hold them both. And thou didst give Behemoth one of the parts which had been dried up on the third day, to live in it, where there are a thousand mountains; but to Leviathan thou didst give the seventh part, the watery part; and thou hast kept them to be eaten by whom thou wilt, and when thou wilt. (2 Esdras 6:49–52)

On that day, two monsters will be parted—one monster, a female named Leviathan, in order to dwell in the abyss of the ocean over the fountains of water; and (the other), a male called Behemoth, which holds his chest in an invisible desert whose name is Dundayin, east of the garden of Eden, wherein the elect and the righteous ones dwell, wherein my grandfather was taken, the seventh from Adam, the first man whom the Lord of the Spirits created. Then I asked the second angel in order that he may show me (how) strong these monsters are, how they were separated on this day and were cast, the one into the abysses of the ocean, and the other into the dry desert. (1 Enoch 60:7–9)

And Behemoth will reveal itself from its place, and Leviathan will come from the sea, the two great monsters which I created on the fifth day of creation and which I shall have kept until that time. And they will be nourishment for all who are left. (2 Baruch 29:4)

Are Behemoth and Leviathan dinosaurs? Were they mythological? The leading proposals are a hippopotamus (Behemoth) and a crocodile (Leviathan). Marvin Pope preferred a buffalo (Behemoth).[114]

Reasonable curiosity about the identity of Behemoth and Leviathan can overshadow the point that God makes through them. Using description and questions, God extolled their physical prowess in order to challenge Job.

> Can anyone capture [Behemoth] when he is on watch, with barbs, can anyone pierce his nose? (Job 40:24)

> Can you draw out Leviathan with a fishhook? Or press down his tongue with a cord? Can you put a rope in his nose? Or pierce his jaw with a hook? Will he make many supplications to you? Or will he speak to you soft words? Will he make a covenant with you? Will you take him for a servant forever? Will you play with him as with a bird? Or will you bind him for your maidens? (41:1–5)

Behemoth and Leviathan were mortal, like Job. All three had been created (40:15), but they were not created equal. God asserted that Behemoth "rank[ed] first among the works of God" (v. 19 NIV). Leviathan sported the title "king over all the sons of pride" (41:34). God added, "Nothing on earth is its equal—a creature without fear" (v. 33 NIV); "no one is so fierce that he dares to arouse him" (v. 10). God thus asked Job, "Who then is he that can stand before Me?" (v. 10). If Job couldn't handle Behemoth nor Leviathan, how could he "manhandle" their Creator?

God Is Free: The Application

At the dedication of the temple, Solomon prayed, "Will God indeed dwell on the earth? Behold, heaven and the highest heaven cannot contain you; how much less this house that I have built!" (1 Kings 8:27). Centuries later, God, through Isaiah, reminded Israel, "Heaven is My throne, and the earth is My footstool. Where then is a house you could build for Me? And where is a place that I may rest?" (Isaiah 66:1).

That God cannot be cornered, boxed, or leashed is a theological "no-brainer." What does not make sense is why I try anyway. Of course, I am speaking metaphorically. My attempts to manipulate God are never overt, always camouflaged; for example, a persistent request prayed confidently or a good deed with strings attached or a scriptural promise quoted word-for-word out of context.

My attempts have never succeeded. That is good news for you *and* me. It confirms that God is God, not a human concoction. The manmade deities behave like their creators, impressed with the theatrics of Baal worshipers on Mount Carmel (1 Kings 18:25–29), bribed if the sacrifice is big enough (Micah 6:6–7), or worn down by meaningless repetition (Matthew 6:7).

Because God is free, only bound by His impeccable character, He always does what is right eternally, not what is expedient in the heat of the moment. He always does what is best for His glory, not just for a vocal minority or the silent majority. He is never a pushover for whoever is most crafty, creative, or clever. You and I, therefore, can approach Him as is. We should be praying, "Thy kingdom come. Thy will be done in earth, as it is in heaven" (Matthew 6:10 KJV).

Thoughts to Ponder

"And going a little farther [Jesus] fell on his face and prayed, saying 'My Father, if it be possible, let this cup pass from me; nevertheless, not as I will, but as you will.'" (Matthew 26:39 ESV)

"Now to Him who is able to do exceeding abundantly beyond all that we ask or think, according to the power that works within us." (Ephesians 3:20)

22

Responding Well When God Confronts

*J*eopardy! first aired on March 30, 1964. The original host of this television show was Art Fleming, not Alex Trebek.

The classic American game show has had highs and lows. It was cancelled twice in the 1970s before its current incarnation which began September 10, 1984, with Trebek as the iconic host until he succumbed to cancer.[115]

What Merv Griffin conceived has never changed. *Jeopardy!* is an atypical quiz show. It gives contestants the answer and requires them to ask the corresponding question.

During the Cycles of Dialogue, Job had questioned God's character, specifically His justice. When God finally responded, He didn't answer the charge. He questioned the questioner. Surprisingly, His questions provided the answers that Job needed.

Watch Your Tone!

The Yahweh Speeches have received a lot of scholarly scrutiny. The reviews are not all positive.

Those who insist that the book of Job is about suffering express their dissatisfaction with what God *did not* say. He never mentioned suffering, Job's or anyone else's. Are the Yahweh Speeches, therefore, irrelevant? If so, why? Was God just out of touch or, worse, the politician who avoids the subject?

Charles Williams, one of the "Inklings," crafted the following conversation in his 1949 novel *War in Heaven*:

> "I'm afraid," the Vicar said gloomily, "this interest in what they call the occult is growing. It's a result of the lack of true religion in these days and a wrong curiosity."
>
> "Oh, wrong, do you think?" Mornington asked. "Would you say any kind of curiosity was wrong? What about Job?"
>
> "Job?" the Archdeacon asked.
>
> "Well, sir, I always understood that where Job scored over the three friends was in feeling a natural curiosity why all those unfortunate things happened to him. They simply put up with it, but he, so to speak, asked God what He thought He was doing."
>
> The Vicar shook his head. "He was told he couldn't understand."
>
> "He was taunted with not being able to understand—which isn't quite the same thing,"
>
> Mornington answered. "As a mere argument there's something lacking perhaps, in saying to a man who's lost his money and his house and his family and is sitting on the dustbin, all over boils, 'Look at the hippopotamus.'"[116]

How God said what He said has upset more people. A blitz-krieg of questions for a sick, grieving, impoverished man seems excessive. Is it not a needless show of force? "Compared to the speeches of Job and the friends, interrogatives are twice as prominent in the speeches of God."[117]

Remarks juxtaposed to some of the questions in the First Yahweh Speech further erode perceptions of God.

First Instance

38:4a	QUESTION	Where were you when I laid the foundation of the earth?
38:4b	REMARK	Tell Me, if you have understanding.

Second Instance

38:16–18a	QUESTIONS	Have you entered into the springs of the sea? Or have you walked in the recesses of the deep? Have the gates of death been revealed to you? Or have you seen the gates of deep darkness? Have you understood the expanse of the earth?
38:18b	REMARK	Tell Me, if you know all this.

Third Instance

38:19–20	QUESTIONS	Where is the way to the dwelling of light? And darkness, where is its place, that you may take it to its territory, and that you may discern the paths to its home?
38:21	REMARK	You know, for you were born then, and the number of your days is great!

Questions + Remarks in the First Yahweh Speech

The best way to assess these criticisms, whether fair or unfair, is to consult Job himself. At the time, no human being cared more about what God would say; Job was desperate. No one else, then or now, could be a better judge of God's words; Job knew immediately if he had been helped. The rest of us are just spectators with an opinion.

In chapter 42, Job responded a second time to the Yahweh Speeches.

I know that you can do all things, and that no purpose of yours can be thwarted. Who is this that hides counsel without knowledge? Therefore I have uttered what I did not understand, things too wonderful for me, which I did not know. "Hear, and I will speak; I will question you, and you make it known to me." I had heard of you by the hearing of the ear, but now my eye sees you; therefore I despise myself, and repent in dust and ashes. (vv. 2–6 ESV)

Reading these words makes sense literally but psychoanalyzing Job is tempting (e.g., *Answer to Job* by Carl Jung). Is he, according to Elisabeth Kubler-Ross, at acceptance (stage five)[118] or manifesting Battered Wife Syndrome? If the Yahweh Speeches are nothing but verbal abuse, then anything Job said about them cannot be trusted. Our criminal justice system would throw out his confession as coerced.

Job, in verses 4–5, sounded like a satisfied student. He hadn't received a letter grade or course credit; so, he must have reacted to what he had learned, spiritual truths that God imparted through lots of questions, a methodology that my colleagues and I in academia still use because they work.

Questions aren't always instructive, the reason that a number of scholars complain that God intimidated, overwhelmed, silenced, humbled, or reprimanded Job. David Robertson, for example, argued,

> While God may be more powerful than we are, he is beneath us on scales that measure love, justice, and wisdom. So we know of him what we know of all tyrants, that while they may torture us and finally kill us, they cannot destroy our personal integrity. From this fact we take our comfort.[119]

Robertson and likeminded critics assume that reading God's questions is the same as Job hearing them, a significant miscalculation. Spoken words, unlike printed ones, have a nonverbal component (e.g., posture, gestures, touch, eye contact, and facial expressions). Spoken words also possess a more nuanced tone than an exclamation mark or a question mark can convey.

> **Biblical Hebrew does not have punctuation; conjunctive and disjunctive accents direct how one reads the text.**

Though none of us can relive Job's audible encounter with God, clues in both speeches do reveal God's tone. The First Yahweh Speech employs overstatement twice.

> Who set its measurements, *since you know*? (38:5, italics mine)

> You know, *for you were born then, and the number of your days is great*! (v. 21, italics mine)

The Second Yahweh Speech employs understatement.

Techniques to Capture Behemoth and Leviathan

> Can anyone capture [Behemoth] when he is on watch, with barbs can anyone pierce his nose? Can you draw out Leviathan with a fishhook? Or press down his tongue with a cord? Can you put a rope in his nose? Or pierce his jaw with a hook? . . . Will the traders bargain over him? Will they divide him among the merchants? Can you fill his skin with harpoons, or his head with fishing spears? (40:24; 41:1–2, 6–7)

Ways to Socialize with Leviathan

> Will he make many supplications to you? Or will he speak to you soft words? Will he make a covenant with you? Will you take him for a servant forever? Will you play

with him as with a bird? Or will you bind him for your maidens? (41:3–5)

Overstatement and understatement are examples of verbal irony, a tension in what is expressed: content vs. intent. Overstatement "says more than it means" whereas understatement "says less than it means."[120]

You and I are more familiar with circumstantial irony, a tension between expectation and reality with some degree of unawareness. Remember Sophocles's *Oedipus Rex* or O' Henry's *The Gift of the Magi*? Consider two examples from Job.[121]

JOB'S SECOND MONOLOGUE

- Expectation Unaware
  I cry to you for help and you do not answer me; I stand, and you only look at me. You have turned cruel to me; with the might of your hand you persecute me. You lift me up on the wind; you make me ride on it, and you toss me about in the roar of the storm. (30:20–22 ESV)
- Reality
  When God finally spoke, He revealed Himself to Job through a storm.

JOB'S FIRST RESPONSE TO BILDAD

- Expectation Unaware
  How shall a man be right with God? If he desired to contend with God, he could not answer him once out of a thousand times. How much more can I answer him? Can I choose my words with him? Though I were righteous, I cannot answer. Instead, I

would implore the favor of my judge. If I called and
he answered me, I cannot believe that he would give
ear to my voice. With a tempest, he would bruise
me and multiply my wounds without cause. For he
is not a man like me that I can answer him. (9:2–3,
14–17, 32, my translation)

- Reality
  When God finally spoke, He revealed Himself to
  Job through a storm. He asked a lot of questions
  that Job couldn't answer.

If God's tone was ironic, then what He said wasn't as harsh as
it appears. Granted, typed irony looks like mockery, taunting, sarcasm, or scorn, but irony is never confrontational. Thus, God did
not raise Job's defenses; the sufferer remained teachable. Refrain-
ing from name-calling and finger-pointing, God enabled Job to
see his own ignorance and inabilities (self-discovery is preferable).
One question was not enough, but eighty-four questions were!

> First Yahweh Speech (38:1-40:2) = 58 questions; Second Yahweh
> Speech (40:6-41:34) = 26 questions

Questions Can Be Answers

God imitated an Ancient Near Eastern sage conducting class.
Answering a question with a question is a traditional Jewish pro-
pensity.[122] One of God's objectives was that Job would come to
his senses—like the prodigal son (Luke 15:17)—but introspection
would not have been enough. To know God better was the lesson;
it always is (Philippians 3:8–10).

Every question highlighted God's knowledge or God's power
at work; attention-getting, therefore, for Job, whose grievance had

been how God wielded omniscience and omnipotence, a recurring theme in seven of his ten speeches.

Job's Speech	References
1st	3:23b
3rd	9:3–12, 19a; 10:8–12, 16
4th	12:9–10, 13–25; 14:1–6, 18–22
7th	21:22
8th	23:6a, 13–14; 24:22–25
9th	26:5–14
10th	30:18–23; 31:15

Theme: God's Alleged Misuse of Omniscience and Omnipotence

Through questions, God showed Job what interests no one for long: remote places like the ocean floor (Job 38:8–11, 16–18) and the desert (vv. 25–27), peculiar creatures like the ostrich (39:13–18) and Behemoth (40:15–24). The disparity could not be greater between what humans ignore that God cares about.

Through questions, Job saw what is unnoticed: God's knowledge and power on behalf of creation's "least of these." If God proved trustworthy with lesser things, when no one was watching, then Job could trust Him. A God with no ulterior motives (e.g., trying to impress others) should be worshiped.

To Be Questioned

During my twenty-four-year career as a college professor, I have stressed thousands of students. I assure you that I'm not sadistic. Quizzes, tests, and papers are inherently stressful.

I have never had a student write me a thank you note for an exam. Don't laugh! I don't expect one. I certainly don't expect what Job did. He worshiped his questioner.

> I know that you can do anything and no plan of yours can be thwarted. You asked, "Who is this who conceals my counsel with ignorance?" Surely I spoke about things I did not understand, things too wondrous for me to know. (42:2–3 CSB)

God's questions revealed just enough about Himself to restore Job's faith. As a result, Job's response to the Second Yahweh Speech concluded with an unconditional surrender: "I take back everything I said, and I sit in dust and ashes to show my repentance" (v. 6 NLT).

The first verb in verse 6 is transitive. "Transitive" grammatically refers to a verb whose action involves a direct or indirect object or both, but an object does not follow *ma'as*, translated "take back" (NLT), "retract" (NASB), "reject" (CSB), "abhor" (KJV, NKJV), or "despise" (NIV, ESV). English translators supply one.

I take back *everything I said* (NLT).

I reject *my words* (CSB).

I abhor *myself* (KJV, NKJV).

I despise *myself* (NIV, ESV).

In English Bibles, the direct object "everything I said," "words," or "myself" will be italicized because it does not occur in the original (Hebrew) text.

Albeit implied, the better reading of verse 6 is that Job retracted his lawsuit. His charges had been baseless, tainted by ulterior motive: a failed attempt to manipulate God. The verb *ma'as* appears seventy-five other times in the Old Testament. It is never reflexive; i.e., accompanied by a pronoun like "myself," "himself," "yourself," or "themselves."

After the Answer

Biblical Hebrew, unlike modern Hebrew, does not have a verb that means "to entertain." Even if it did, God would not have been a subject. To amuse is never His objective because the typical reactions (e.g., laughter, astonishment, shock, and excitement) do not last, thus cannot change a life. Whenever God does act, you and I need to be ready to respond appropriately. The Bible is proof that He is willing to show us His glory (Exodus 33:18–34:7) if we are willing to praise and worship (34:8), to trust and obey.

Thoughts to Ponder

"Behold, how happy is the man whom God reproves, so do not despise the discipline of the Almighty." (Job 15:17)

"So Eli told Samuel, 'Go and lie down, and if he calls you, say, "Speak, Lord, for your servant is listening."'" (1 Samuel 3:9 NIV)

"Do not despise the Lord's instruction, my son, and do not loathe his discipline." (Proverbs 3:11 CSB)

23

Distinguishing Knowledge and Answers

Why do you want to go to heaven? Of course, seeing Jesus is the number one reason (Philippians 1:21–23). Why else do you want to go to heaven?

- reuniting with family and friends or meeting that legendary relative for the first time
- having a lengthy conversation with a Bible character
- never saying "good-bye" or "see you later" again
- no more tears, death, or pain (Revelation 21:4)
- no Satan
- no sin
- no more stress because of a lack of time
- getting a new body (1 Corinthians 15:50–58)
- eating without worrying about calories or cholesterol

- enjoying new skills, talents, and abilities like singing or walking through walls
- experiencing perfection finally

For every generation, heaven provides hope, a future of unlimited possibilities. Limited information about it stirs fascination as well as frustration. The apostle Paul, quoting the prophet Isaiah, wrote, "No eye has seen, nor ear has heard, no mind has imagined what God has prepared for those who love him" (1 Corinthians 2:9 NLT).

Heaven's mystique encourages imaginations to run wild; for example, the expectation of being a know-it-all: "When I get to heaven, I'll know _____ ." While the options are endless, here are a few one might use to fill in the blank.

- if Apollo 11 really landed on the moon
- who shot John F. Kennedy
- when and how the world began
- what happened at Area 51
- why the Mayans disappeared
- if dogs and cats actually think
- who fired first at Lexington, the British or the colonists
- how the Egyptians built the pyramids
- where Amelia Earhart crashed
- if Bigfoot is a myth

In his definitive work on heaven, Randy Alcorn explained, "God alone is omniscient. When we die, we'll see things far more clearly, and we'll know much more than we do now, but we'll *never* know everything."[123]

On earth, outside of academia, brilliance both impresses and disappoints. Knowing a "what" like quantum physics, microbiology, or chemical engineering can earn one the distinction "expert" without having the expertise to answer any of life's whys, such as:

- Why did my mom and dad divorce?
- Why hasn't God answered my prayers for full-time employment?
- Why doesn't a person who does the crime always do the time?
- Why did God allow COVID-19 to cancel mission trips?
- Though church involvement was a family priority, why has my son rebelled?
- Why did the neighbor's tree miss their house but crush ours?
- Why hasn't revival taken place?
- Why did an uninsured driver total our car?
- Why does the devil *still* "steal and kill and destroy"?
- While others terminate their unwanted pregnancies, why can't I conceive?

After the two rounds of tragedy, Job wanted to know why (answers). What his friends were offering (theological knowledge) failed to satisfy him.

Why Not Ask Why?

"Instinctive" describes an action or reaction that occurs without thinking. Saying "Ouch!" is an instant response to injury. To duck without looking follows hearing a loud sound overhead. Closing one's eyes happens simultaneously when sneezing.

To ask "why?" after a misfortune is instinctive too. Job did so more than once.

Why did I not die at birth, come forth from the womb and expire? (Job 3:11)

Why is light given to him who suffers, and life to the bitter of soul; who long for death, but there is none, and dig for it more than for hidden treasures; who rejoice greatly, they exult when they find the grave? Why is light given to a man whose way is hidden, and whom God has hedged in? (vv. 20–23)

If I sin, what do I do to you, you watcher of mankind? Why have you made me your mark? Why have I become a burden to you? Why do you not pardon my transgression and take away my iniquity? For now I shall lie in the earth; you will seek me, but I shall not be. (7:20–21 ESV)

I will say to God, do not condemn me; let me know why you contend against me. Does it seem good to you to oppress, to despise the work of your hands and favor the designs of the wicked? (10:2–3 ESV)

Why did you bring me out from the womb? (v. 18 ESV)

Why do you hide your face and count me as your enemy? (13:24 ESV)

Why do the wicked live, reach old age, and grow mighty in power? (21:7 ESV)

Why are not times of judgment kept by the Almighty, and why do those who know him never see his days? (24:1 ESV)

"Why" is not necessarily a bad question. It is a way to vent anger and frustration or to get perspective, but it oftentimes yields no reply. What humans cannot answer, God may choose not to answer. Unanswered questions can fester, becoming a distraction or, worse, eroding peace of mind.

Warning: God May Answer!

Habakkuk, like Job, asked God why. Wicked countrymen (ungodly) running rampant had upset the seventh-century prophet.

O Lord, how long shall I cry for help, and you will not hear? Or cry to you "Violence!" and you will not save? Why do you make me see iniquity, and why do you idly look at wrong? Destruction and violence are before me; strife and contention arise. So the law is paralyzed, and justice never goes forth. For the wicked surround the righteous; so justice goes forth perverted. (Habakkuk 1:2–4 ESV)

Because God chose to answer promptly, Habakkuk did not need patience. A chair, on the other hand, would have been nice to absorb the shock. God announced,

Look among the nations, and see; wonder and be astounded. For I am doing a work in your days that you would not believe if told. For behold, I am raising up the Chaldeans, that bitter and hasty nation, who march through the breadth of the earth, to seize dwellings not their own. They are dreaded and fearsome; their justice and dignity go forth from themselves. Their horses are swifter than leopards, more fierce than the evening wolves; their horsemen press proudly on. Their horsemen come from afar; they fly like an eagle swift to devour. They all come for violence, all their faces forward. They gather captives like sand. At kings they scoff, and at rulers they laugh. They laugh at every fortress, for they pile up earth and take it. Then they sweep by like the wind and go on, guilty men, whose own might is their god! (vv. 5–11 ESV)

An invasion of pagans (godless) provoked the prophet to ask why again.

Are you not from everlasting, O Lord my God, my Holy One? We shall not die. O Lord, you have ordained them as a judgment, and you, O Rock, have established them for reproof. You who are of purer eyes than to see evil and cannot look at wrong, why do you idly look at traitors and remain silent when the wicked swallows up the man more righteous than he? (vv. 12–13 ESV)

When God answered Habakkuk again, His lengthier reply (2:3–20) concluded, "The Lord is in His holy temple. Let all the earth be silent before Him."

Questions can start a meaningful conversation, but ultimately, they impede our being where God wants us: worshiping in His presence. Questioners are not worshipers, but they can become one.

Read Habakkuk 3. It is nineteen verses but NO whys. It records the prophet's praise; what God had patiently awaited. Habakkuk's testimony concluded:

> I heard and my inward parts trembled, at the sound my lips quivered. Decay enters my bones, and in my place I tremble. Because I must wait quietly for the day of distress, for the people to arise who will invade us. Though the fig tree should not blossom, and there be no fruit on the vines, though the yield of the olive should fail, and the fields produce no food, though the flock should be cut off from the fold, and there be no cattle in the stalls, yet I will exult in the Lord. I will rejoice in the God of my salvation. The Lord God is my strength, and He has made my feet like hinds' feet, and makes me walk on my high places. (3:16–19)

And the Answer, Job, Is . . .

Job may have waited longer than Habakkuk, but God did answer: two lengthy replies. Neither speech, however, met Job's expectations. God never addressed any of Job's whys. He did ask a lot of questions (no whys). He did not tackle the topic of suffering.

Oh, to have seen Job's face. The storm surely startled him until God started speaking. His anticipation then heightened until God's questions piled up. Disappointment swiftly ensued, dictating Job's First Response.

> Behold, I have been slighted by you. How then could I return to you? My hand, I put upon my mouth. I have spoken once, but I will not answer; even twice, but I will not add again. (Job 40:4–5, my translation)

Paraphrasing Job, "I cannot answer Your questions, but You have not answered mine!"

God undeterred resumed His questioning. The effect was drastically different. Job's Second Response begins with a doxology (42:2) and ends with an unconditional surrender (v. 6). A confession of ignorance (vv. 3–5) connects them.

Twice, Job spoke the Hebrew verb *yada*, translated "to know." It is how he humbled himself, the prerequisite in order to worship God.

> *I know* that you can do anything and no plan of yours can be thwarted. You asked, "Who is this who conceals my counsel with ignorance?" Surely I spoke about things I did not understand, things too wondrous for me *to know* [italics mine]. (vv. 2–3 CSB)

Twice, Job expressed a contrast.

Theological Accuracy
What he had thought about God compared to what God taught him

Relational Depth
What he knew about God from afar versus in a seat on the front row

The weighty effect of the contrasts moved Job to answer the first and easiest of God's eighty-four questions: "Who is this that darkens counsel by words without knowledge?" (38:2; 42:3). Paraphrasing Job, "Guilty as charged!"

Attention, Please!

Like any question, "why" fosters listening because it fine-tunes attention: the expectation of an answer. Hope sustains patience until the answer hopefully comes.

One of our faults as human beings is how we define "answer." It isn't a reasonable response; it must be a favorable one. The boss, for example, may ask rather than order, even give extra time to think about it, but don't be fooled! Your superior awaits an affirmative. Oftentimes, the praying Christian is no better; of course, an answer to prayer is a "Yes."

Job could have rejected God's speeches as words but not answers because God did not say what he had wanted to hear. Instead, Job worshiped again—compare 42:1–6 to 1:20–21. What he received exceeded his expectations. God had delivered a personalized portion of knowledge. Moreover, Job learned that God values the questioner more than we humans value our questions.

Thoughts to Ponder

"It is the glory of God to conceal a matter." (Proverbs 25:2)

"Many of our questions—especially those that begin with the word *why*—will have to remain unanswered for the time being."[124] (James Dobson)

"Be still, and know that I am God. I will be exalted among the nations, I will be exalted in the earth!" (Psalm 46:10 ESV)

"For who has understood the mind of the Lord so as to instruct him?" (1 Corinthians 2:16 ESV)

24

Thinking before Speaking:
"Thus Saith the Lord"

Proverbs 31 consists of two sections, verses 1–9 and 10–31. The second section, a Hebrew acrostic, is the more famous, profiling a "godly woman" or an "excellent wife." The first section, according to verse 1, is "The words of King Lemuel, the oracle which his mother taught him." In it, verse 8 states, "Speak up for those who cannot speak for themselves, for the rights of all who are destitute" (NIV). The "destitute" are probably orphans. The Hebrew text literally reads "left-behind sons."[125]

Children were vulnerable in the Ancient Near East (they still are worldwide). That society placed more value on age, the older the better.

I am young in years, and you are aged; therefore I was timid and afraid to declare my opinion to you. I said, "Let days speak, and many years teach wisdom." But it is the spirit in man, the breath of the Almighty that makes him understand. It is not the old who are wise, nor the aged who understand what is right. Therefore I say, "Listen to me; let me also declare my opinion." (Job 32:6–10 ESV)

Let no one look down on your youthfulness, but rather in speech, conduct, love, faith and purity, show yourself an example of those who believe. (1 Timothy 4:12)

In contrast, God has never been vulnerable. He knows how to communicate. He can speak for Himself with a forceful voice, moving Elihu to marvel,

At this also my heart trembles, and leaps from its place. Listen closely to the thunder of His voice, and the rumbling that goes out from His mouth. Under the whole heaven He lets it loose, and His lightning to the ends of the earth. After it, a voice roars; He thunders with His majestic voice; and He does not restrain the lightnings when His voice is heard. God thunders with His voice wondrously, doing great things which we cannot comprehend. (Job 37:1–5)

Nevertheless, God routinely enlists spokespersons: in the biblical time period, prophets declared His words; when the church began, apostles, evangelists, and pastors became His mouthpiece.

The first prophet was Abraham (Genesis 20:7). In Genesis 18, during a brief conversation with God, he repeatedly expressed a trepidation to say anything.

Now that I have been so bold as to speak to the Lord, though I am nothing but dust and ashes. (v. 27 NIV)

May the Lord not be angry, but let me speak. (v. 30 NIV)

Now that I have been so bold as to speak to the Lord. (v. 31 NIV)

May the Lord not be angry, but let me speak just once more. (v. 32 NIV)

Such reverence for God is wisdom. "Fools rush in where angels fear to tread."[126] Being casual, cavalier, or overconfident (lit., presumptuously, according to Deuteronomy 18) is a pre-existing condition of false prophets.

Before You Speak a Word . . .

To prophesy falsely was a capital offense in Israel (Deuteronomy 18:20). Elijah, therefore, slew four hundred prophets of the Canaanite fertility god Baal (1 Kings 18:40). When Jeremiah and a false prophet named Hananiah clashed, God backed His prophet, instructing Jeremiah to pronounce the following judgment:

Listen now, Hananiah, the Lord has not sent you, and you have made this people trust in a lie. Therefore thus says the Lord, "Behold, I am about to remove you from the face of the earth. This year you are going to die, because you have counseled rebellion against the Lord." (Jeremiah 28:15–16)

Jeremiah 28 concludes, "So Hananiah the prophet died in the same year in the seventh month" (v. 17).

Why false prophets anger God is not a mystery; at least three reasons can be cited.

1. God is truth; because lies contradict who He is, He Himself cannot lie (Numbers 23:19; 1 Samuel 15:29; 2 Timothy 2:13; Titus 1:2; Hebrews 6:18).

2. Lies, without exception, negatively impact whoever believes them. The result can be fatal (e.g., man of God in 1 Kings 13; King Ahab in 1 Kings 22).

3. God is jealous about His name (Exodus 20:7; Ezekiel 39:25); hence, He combats any message that mischarac-

terizes Him—bearing His name but not conveying His words.

How God regards false prophets explains His rebuke of Eliphaz, Bildad, and Zophar: "My anger burns against you and against your two friends, for you have not spoken of me what is right, as my servant Job has" (Job 42:7 ESV).

In the story, God is talked about more than any other character. Job, Job's friends, and Elihu did almost all of the talking.

Elihu spoke last. His four speeches glorified God, but God did not acknowledge what he said; no one did.

Job spoke first. In the Prologue, he was a worshiper. After the Prologue, he became an outspoken critic and litigant. His verbal assaults (ten speeches) warranted the Yahweh Speeches.

Job's friends only spoke during the Cycles of Dialogue. They were well-versed in traditional theology, devout like Saul who had been zealous as "a persecutor of the church" (Philippians 3:6). To upset God would have mortified Eliphaz, Bildad, and Zophar; how Saul surely felt after Jesus confronted him on the Damascus Road (Acts 9:1–9).

Only Eliphaz heard God's displeasure because God addressed him as the "group leader," holding him more accountable.

> Now therefore take seven bulls and seven rams and go to my servant Job and offer up a burnt offering for yourselves. And my servant Job shall pray for you, for I will accept his prayer not to deal with you according to your folly. For you have not spoken of me what is right, as my servant Job has. (Job 42:8 ESV)

During the Cycles of Dialogue, Eliphaz always spoke before Bildad or Zophar, an indication that he outranked them.

The punishment itself shows how angry God was with all three. The blood of seven bulls and seven rams could cover the sins of a nation (1 Chronicles 15:26; Ezekiel 45:21–25). Without Job's intercession, however, it would not have been enough.

"As My servant Job has," a repeated comment, can be an interpretive distraction. Was not Job also disrespectful or, worse, blasphemous? To what did God refer? The best answer is what Job said last: a brief response (Job 42:1–6) that offsets ten speeches; proof that God has a "short" memory, that what you and I do lately matters more.

The friends' folly should be the focus. What was it? The Hebrew noun *neᵇbala*, translated "folly," occurs twelve additional times in the Old Testament, referring to words (Isaiah 9:17; 32:6) as well as deeds; for example, sexual assault (Genesis 34:7; Judges 19:23–24; 2 Samuel 13:12) and Achan's calamitous disobedience at Jericho (Joshua 7:15).[127]

God specifically denounced what Eliphaz, Bildad, and Zophar had spoken about Him (theology), not what they had spoken about Job. In contrast, Job disagreed with everything they said, even how they said it.

> Doubtless you are the only people who matter, and wisdom will die with you! But I have a mind as well as you; I am not inferior to you. Who does not know all these things? (Job 12:2–3 NIV; see also 13:2)

> You are worthless physicians, all of you! If only you would be altogether silent! For you, that would be wisdom. (13:4–5 NIV)

> I have heard many such things; sorry comforters are you all. Is there no limit to windy words? Or what plagues you that you answer? I too could speak like you, if I were

in your place. I could compose words against you, and shake my head at you. (16:2–4)

How long will you torment me, and crush me with words? These ten times you have insulted me, you are not ashamed to wrong me. (19:2–3)

Listen carefully to my speech, and let this be your way of consolation. Bear with me that I may speak; then after I have spoken, you may mock. (21:2–3)

What a help you are to the weak! How you have saved the arm without strength! What counsel you have given to one without wisdom! What helpful insight you have abundantly provided! To whom have you uttered words? And whose spirit was expressed through you? (26:2–4)

Job's response to Zophar's first speech was actually prophetic.

Will you speak what is unjust for God, and speak what is deceitful for Him? Will you show partiality for Him? Will you contend for God? Will it be well when He examines you? Or will you deceive Him as one deceives a man? He will surely reprove you, if you secretly show partiality. Will not His majesty terrify you, and the dread of Him fall on you? Your memorable sayings are proverbs of ashes, your defenses are defenses of clay. (13:7–12)

Eliphaz, Bildad, and Zophar had spouted Deuteronomic Theology exclusively, the gist of the Proverbs. Their beliefs, therefore, were not heretical. Their error was how they had applied them, presuming to know how God was handling Job. Even we the readers know how wrong they were.

No Margin for Error

At the royal palace, where he enjoyed the best view of Jerusalem, David conversed with Nathan the prophet. The king noted the obvious: "See now, I dwell in a house of cedar, but the ark of God dwells within tent curtains" (2 Samuel 7:2).

Nathan knew his lord well enough to hear much more than a statement. David had expressed an intent to shelter the ark better and he awaited the feedback of his trusted counselor. Nathan obliged without consulting God: "Go, do all that is in your mind, *for the Lord is with you* [italics mine]" (v. 3). The prophet should have known better.

Before that day ended, the word of the Lord came to Nathan, a twelve-verse message (vv. 5–16) that David should have heard. Nathan, trying to be supportive, had meant well, but he immediately became a false prophet when his opinion pretended to be God's will.

Good intentions do not impress God. What matters to Him, whenever speaking on His behalf, is exactness. Before Jeremiah delivered the famous "Temple Sermon," God reminded him, "Speak . . . all the words that I have commanded you to speak to them. Do not omit a word!" (Jeremiah 26:2)

God's staunch stance is why James cautioned, "Let not many of you become teachers, my brethren, knowing that as such we shall incur a stricter judgment" (James 3:1). God isn't petty, but He does care about details. He isn't a perfectionist even though He is eternally perfect. Messaging, for Him, is personal. God wants to be known rightly; His objective is a personal relationship with us: the miracle of finite creatures intimately bonding with an infinite being.

Sadly, we are prone to misunderstand. For us to know God, therefore, requires Him to overcome our sinful flesh and cognitive limitations. He does! His efforts to reveal Himself have been herculean: "The Word became flesh, and dwelt among us" (John 1:14).

Sadly, we lack the spiritual maturity to discern consistently what is true. It should be a priority because the "father of lies" (John 8:44) wars against God, conducting a misinformation campaign. It is his obsession.

Scripture documents how the devil mischaracterizes God.

1. Invoking His Name

In Eden, the serpent asked Eve, "Has God said?" (Genesis 3:1)

2. Misapplying His Word

In the wilderness, as part of his attempt to tempt Jesus, Satan quoted Psalm 91 out of context (Matthew 4:5–6; Luke 4:9–11).

You and I can become the unwitting mouth of the misinformation campaign, doing the devil's dirty work, if we trust what we know more than whom we should know. Failing to spot that misplaced confidence will hurt us. Because souls lie in the balance, God does not tolerate being misrepresented, no matter who is responsible, friend or foe. In the book of Job, friends exacerbated Job's suffering by weaponizing theology.

Thoughts to Ponder

"'But this is the covenant that I will make with the house of Israel after those days,' declares the Lord: 'I will put my law within them, and I will write it on their hearts. And I will be their God, and they shall be my people. And no longer shall each one teach his neighbor and each his brother, saying, "Know the Lord," for they shall all know me, from the least of them to the greatest,' declares the Lord." (Jeremiah 31:33-34 ESV)

"And as for you, the anointing which you received from Him abides in you, and you have no need for anyone to teach you; but as His anointing teaches you about all things, and is true and is not a lie, and just as it has taught you, you abide in Him." (1 John 2:27)

"For the earth will be filled with the knowledge of the glory of the Lord as the waters cover the sea." (Habakkuk 2:14)

"Christ has no hands but our hands to do His work today;

He has no feet but our feet to lead men in His way;

He has no tongue but our tongues to tell men how He died;

He has no help but our help to bring them to His side."[128] (Annie Johnson Flint)

"We shouldn't speak with an assurance we don't really have like we're God's PR agent and risk misquoting the God of the universe, who could turn us into a pile of salt. This all helps me be a little more respectful and humble when I'm attributing something to God."[129] (Bob Goff)

25

Testifying God Is *Still* in Control

What are your memories of English grammar? Have you recovered? I recall diagramming sentences in sixth grade. Was it wise to arm eleven- and twelve-year-old boys with rulers? I also remember Mrs. Harmon's ninth grade English class. Her lectures were clear, even captivating, until the moment she said, "predicate nominative" and "predicate adjective." Why were my ears hearing the forbidden words of an ancient tongue, extinct for thousands of years?

Throughout grade school, science and math were my favorite subjects. ACT and SAT scores attest that English wasn't. In fact, English grammar didn't interest me until I took French, German, Greek, Hebrew, and Latin. I would not have fared well without my English teachers.

Now, teaching biblical Hebrew, I urge my college students to review English grammar, especially the parts of speech. Understanding that words have function (syntax) as well as meaning (sense) is necessary in order to translate.

"Adverbs describe the action of verbs and also modify adjectives, other adverbs, and whole groups of words."[130] In English, an -ly ending typically distinguishes this part of speech: e.g., *slowly, recently, quickly, completely, badly, wisely,* and *carefully.*

Adverbs without an -ly ending may be inconspicuous, but they are not uncommon, such as *very, almost, here, again, always, often,* and *still.*

The adverb *still* signifies the passage of time or a persistence. Although a small word, it significantly changes the meaning of a sentence.

Are you eating?
Are you *still* eating?

I love you.
I love you *still.*

She is a college student.
She is *still* a college student.

He has no job.
He *still* has no job.

God is in control.
God is *still* in control.

Not a Disney Ending

Mary Ann and I do not watch many movies together. I like action; she calls it violence. I like horror; nothing about monsters, ghosts, or demons interests her. I like sci-fi; she thinks that aliens are repulsive. Mary Ann likes feel-good; I complain, "So unrealistic!" Undaunted, she asserts that everyday life is enough reality. She prefers "And they lived happily ever after."

The creative folk at Disney have perfected the happy ending accompanied by a catchy tune. They would not have written the book of Job. Its ending is not realistic: Job's praise (Job 42:1–6) *precedes* his restoration (vv. 10–17). Why would anyone worship on an ash heap?

Old Testament scholars criticize how the book of Job ends because they have misread it.

> The Epilogue has been held by many to mar the book, since it is said to give the case away to the friends. Here Job's prosperity is restored, and righteousness finds its reward in happiness, as the friends had said it always did, and as Job had maintained it should. But this seems to miss the point completely.[131]

> Many modern interpreters focus on Job's humbling himself before God in dust and ashes as the conclusion and thus dislike the epilogue as anticlimactic and unrealistic.[132]

The Hebrew words *shub* (verb) and *sh^ebit* (noun), occurring in verse 10, are the key to deciphering verses 10–17: "And the Lord restored [*shub*] the fortune [*sh^ebit*] of Job." Elsewhere, *shub sh^ebit* means the end of captivity and a restoration of favor and blessing (e.g., Psalm 85:10; Jeremiah 29:14).[133] *Shub* by itself does not mean "to reward." Its typical translations are "to turn" or "to return."

| The Hebrew verbs *shalem* and *gamal* can be rendered "to reward."

God restoring Job (lit., returning what had belonged to Job) signaled the end of the test. It should have ended because Job passed, but only God could halt what He allowed the adversary to do. God, in charge, exercised control.

God, in charge, has never been derelict. The evidence is as extensive as eternity; Job had heard just a sampling. Consequently, after the Yahweh Speeches, he worshiped, still suffering: "I know that you can do anything and no plan of yours can be thwarted" (Job 42:2 CSB). The reminder of God's constant, complete control was good enough. The restoration that soon followed, in comparison, was lagniappe (i.e., "a little extra," according to Louisianians).

Passage of Time and Persistence

Circumstances can be good or bad, passing or lasting. How we perceive them can make them better or worse.

Oftentimes, our assessment of the situation lacks key facts, inaccessible for a lot of reasons. Case in point, Job. He yearned for the perspective that we the readers have at our fingertips: specifically, the Prologue. Even when God spoke from the whirlwind, He withheld information that Job would have appreciated.

Our ongoing challenge whenever the senseless or unthinkable happens is not to jump to conclusions but to remind ourselves that God is still in control. Hasn't He earned the benefit of the doubt?

As a Southern Baptist since childhood, I have heard many testimonies. I've even shared a few. It is our tradition. Pastors regularly cede time for congregants to report what God has done in their lives recently; especially, how He has answered a prayer. My mom did not disappoint our pastor or our church. When she stood (all 4'11" of her) to speak, I sunk in the pew because I knew that teardrops would soon fall and squelch her attempt to testify. I'm now embarrassed to admit that I was embarrassed.

Mom embodied the "God is still in control" testimony. Pain and sorrow shadowed her from birth (surviving spinal meningitis) to death (succumbing to a debilitating stroke). At age sixteen, she lost her mother to breast cancer. After age forty-three, lower back pain, rheumatoid arthritis, and lupus diminished her quality of life. At age forty-six, she survived divorce, never to remarry. If you could have met my mom, she would have offered to pray for you. She was a "prayer warrior." You would have heard her praise the Lord because her faith transcended circumstances.

The "God is still in control" testimony emerges after months or years of twists and turns. It is persistence with a voice. Its stage is the ash heap, not the air-conditioned auditorium.

Scripture records plenty of "God is still in control" testimonies. Headed to the land of Moriah, Abraham assured Isaac, the oblivious sacrifice, "God will provide for Himself the lamb for the burnt offering, my son" (Genesis 22:7). Joseph informed his brothers, "And as for you, you meant evil against me, but God meant it for good in order to bring about this present result, to preserve many people alive" (50:20). David sang, "Even though I walk through the valley of the shadow of death, I will fear no evil, for you are with me; your rod and your staff, they comfort me" (Psalm 23:4 ESV). Paul told the Ephesian leadership,

And now, behold, bound in spirit, I am on my way to Jerusalem, not knowing what will happen to me there, except that the Holy Spirit solemnly testifies to me in every city, saying that bonds and afflictions await me. But I do not consider my life of any account as dear to myself, in order that I may finish my course, and the ministry which

204 | **When Life Meets the Soul**

I received from the Lord Jesus, to testify solemnly of the gospel of the grace of God. (Acts 20:22–24)

Everyone spends time on the ash heap. To live long enough is to return there. Of course, it isn't a place that anyone wants to visit, but the platform it provides beats primetime media coverage. If, atop the ash heap, we testify, "God is still in control," the world, not just the church, pays attention. The reason is obvious: Anyone can worship after God doubles his or her belongings. Why would anyone worship on an ash heap?

Thoughts to Ponder

"The steps of a man are established by the Lord, when he delights in his way; though he fall, he shall not be cast headlong, for the Lord upholds his hand. I have been young, and now am old, yet I have not seen the righteous forsaken or his children begging for bread." (Psalm 37:23-25 ESV)

"Had it not been the Lord who was on our side, when men rose up against us; then they would have swallowed us alive, when their anger was kindled against us; then the waters would have engulfed us, the stream would have swept over our soul; then the raging waters would have swept over our soul." (Psalm 124:2-5)

Appendix:

How to Read the Cycles of Dialogue

The Bible is a book of books, a variety of literary genres written over centuries: history, law, song, wisdom, prophecy, gospel, letter, and apocalyptic. Right interpretation (hermeneutics) presupposes that what one reads determines how one reads.

Job is a wisdom book, but its structure and substance are unlike its Hebrew counterparts Proverbs or Ecclesiastes. Job begins and ends with prose (chaps. 1–2; 42:7–17). Its large middle is poetry (3:1–42:6). Dialogue advances its plot.

All three wisdom books more or less defy the standard way to read something: start at the first page and stop after the last page. Proverbs 10–29 is a jumble of sayings, mostly two-liners. The first eleven chapters of Ecclesiastes consist of recurring themes that appear and disappear for no reason. In the Cycles of Dialogue

(Job 4–27), Eliphaz, Bildad, and Zophar talk about the doctrine of divine retribution every time they speak (eight speeches), forcing Job to defend himself again and again.

Table tennis matches do not have a wide appeal. Similarly, the "back and forth" between Job and his friends has frustrated members of academia as well as the church. Old Testament scholar Robert Gordis wrote, "In Job there is no plot from the opening of the debate until its close, with the final appearance of the Lord from the whirlwind and Job's reconciliation with His maker."[134] I, as a pastor, have heard plenty of discouraged saints make the same observation, "The words ran together. My brain started throbbing."

A better way to grasp the Cycles of Dialogue is to group together the speeches of each speaker and then read the speeches in each grouping sequentially.

SPEAKER	SPEECHES: Chapters
Eliphaz	4–5, 15, 22
Bildad	8, 18, 25
Zophar	11, 20
Job	6–7, 9–10, 12–14, 16–17, 19, 21, 23–24, 26–27

Alternative Way to Read the Cycles of Dialogue

Such an approach uncovers the following facts:
1. Speakers did not repeat themes but modified them according to context or an intended emphasis.
2. The arguments of Job's friends became more accusatory.
3. The length of Job's speeches decreased in each successive cycle.
4. Job gradually addressed his friends less.

5. Job steadily addressed God more indirectly (third person) than directly (second person).
6. The length of the friends' speeches decreased in each successive cycle.
7. Job's hope waned in each successive cycle.

Acknowledgments

Thank you, reader. Before your hands ever held this book, it passed through many hands, a slew of contributors.

    In fall 1992, Dr. Wayne VanHorn taught "Old Testament Exegesis of Job" at New Orleans Baptist Theological Seminary. Taking his doctoral seminar changed my life's trajectory: at first, a dissertation on Job, now a book about Job. Years earlier, Drs. George Harrison and Waylon Bailey had taught me biblical Hebrew, qualifying me to be one of Dr. VanHorn's students. I am a living investment of godly professors.

    Each chapter of *When Life Meets the Soul* juxtaposes the details of Job and the experiences of life. My wife and children were my inspirations—codeword for illustrations—a burden that they handle with grace.

    Before and during the publication of *When Life Meets the Soul*, God answered a lot of prayers. I salute my prayer team: Dr. Brent Barker, Mrs. LaJune White, and Mrs. Carol Whitfield.

    The publication of *When Life Meets the Soul* is also the hard work of a lot of people. I am grateful for and indebted to the outstanding team at Morgan James Publishing: David Hancock (CEO), Heidi Nickerson (Author Onboarding Manager), Emily Madison (Author Relations Manager), Jim Howard, Wes Taylor, and Tom Dean. Their expertise *and* encouragement have been exceptional; I needed both. Russell Rankin, my editor, was "iron that sharpens iron." Kent Mummert, a graphic designer, and Bill Watkins, an editor, were my heroes at the eleventh hour. Rich Perspectives (www.richperspectives.com) has handled the huge responsibility of marketing with impeccable professionalism. May the Lord bless Mark Rich, Chrissy Sanders, Chad Cockrell, Clay Meyer, and Clark Kilgore.

The author of Ecclesiastes warned, "The writing of many books is endless, and excessive devotion to books is wearying to the body" (12:12). My experience, however, has compared to an adventure that leads to a fabulous destination with a few unforeseen twists and turns. Drama can be good! I still marvel that God selected an unknown slowpoke for such an assignment as this.

About the Author

Ivan D. Parke, PhD, is a professor in the Department of Christian Studies at Mississippi College where he has taught since 1998. His areas of expertise are Biblical Studies and Biblical Hebrew. Parke's love for the Old Testament began in graduate school, eventually leading him to the wisdom books (Proverbs and Job) and culminating with his dissertation "The Literary Role of the Yahweh Speeches in the Book of Job."

Prior to being a professor, Parke was a pastor in Alabama and a minister of youth in Florida and Louisiana. He still serves the local church as a Bible study leader, retreat speaker, and supply preacher. He has also been the interim pastor at twelve Mississippi churches.

When Life Meets the Soul is Parke's second book. In 2004, he and Larry Garner coauthored *Reclaiming the Real Jesus.*

Parke and his wife Mary Ann live in Jackson, Mississippi. They have two grown children. When he is not writing, teaching, or preaching, he enjoys yardwork, exercising, music, and sports.

Please visit the author's Business page on Facebook.

Additional Resources

Please visit the author's website, www.ivanparke.com for a PowerPoint, handouts, and videos. Are you interested in using *When Life Meets the Soul* as a small group Bible study? If so, a Student Guide as well as a Book of Job Reading Plan are available.

Endnotes

1   Paul R. Ehrlich, Anne H. Ehrlich, and John P. Holdren, *Ecoscience: Population, Resources, Environment* (San Francisco: W. H. Freeman and Company, 1977), 14.

2   Ibid., 97.

3   Jill Briscoe, *It Had to Be a Monday* (Wheaton, IL: Tyndale House Publishers, Inc., 1995), 213.

4   Laurence J. Peter, *Peter's Quotations: Ideas for Our Time* (New York: Quill, 1992), 303.

5   Ibid.

6   Ibid.

7   Ibid., 306.

8   James W. Vander Zanden, *Human Development*, 3rd ed. (New York: Alfred A. Knopf, Inc., 1985), 202.

9   John Naisbitt, *Megatrends: Ten New Directions Transforming Our Lives* (New York: Warner Books, Inc., 1984), 35.

10 See https://www.youtube.com/watch?v=3cobOW_uOjc, accessed July 6, 2021.

11 Nik Ripken, *The Insanity of God: A True Story of Faith Resurrected* (Nashville: B&H Publishing Group, 2013), 86.

12 Calvin Miller, *The Valiant Papers* (Grand Rapids: Zondervan Publishing House, 1982), 27.

13 John Oswalt, *Where are You, God?* (Nappanee, IN: Evangel Publishing House, 1999), 104.

14 Philip Yancey, *The Jesus I Never Knew* (Grand Rapids: Zondervan, 1995), 160.

15 A. W. Tozer, *The Knowledge of the Holy* (New York: Harper & Row, Publishers, 1961), 9.

16 Voltaire, *Le Sottisier*, 32, quoted in *Dictionary of Quotations* (New York: Delacorte Press, 1968), 278.

17 Rudyard Kipling, "The City of Brass," in *The Writings in Prose and Verse of Rudyard Kipling: The Years Between and Poems from History*, vol. 27 (New York: Charles Scribner's Sons, 1919), 124–25.

18 https://literarydevices.net/anthropomorphism, accessed February 17, 2022.

19 Judges 6:25–32; 1 Samuel 5:1–5; Psalm 115:1–8; 135:5–18; Isaiah 40:18–26; 41:1–29; 44:6–20; 45:20–46:11; Jeremiah 10:1–16; Habakkuk 2:18–20.

20 Job 40:10–11; Isaiah 29:15–16; 45:9; Romans 9:19–21.

21 Gregory of Nyssa, *The Life of Moses*, trans. Abraham J. Malherbe and Everett Ferguson (New York: Paulist Press Inc., 1978), 2.165.

22 J. B. Phillips, *Your God Is Too Small* (New York: Macmillan Publishing Co., Inc., 1961), 9.

23 Rick Joyner, *The Final Quest* (New Kensington, PA: Whitaker House, 1996), 155.

24 Don Musser, "Doctor Don's Doings," *The Halifax Herald* 44, no. 3 (18 January 1998): 1.

25 https://www.independent.co.uk/news/world/europe/compulsive-hoarder-crushed-to-death-under-mound-of-rubbish-a6973121.html, accessed July 8, 2021; https://

www.thelocal.es/20160407/hoarder-crushed-death-under-rubbish-garbage-pile-spain, accessed July 8, 2021.

26 Glandion Carney and William Long, *Trusting God Again* (Downers Grove, IL: InterVarsity, Press, 1995), 64.

27 Billy Graham, "Joy in Tribulation," *Decision* 58, no. 11 (November 2017): 22.

28 Paul Brand and Philip Yancey, *Pain: The Gift Nobody Wants* (New York: HarperCollins Publishers, Inc., 1993), 12, 13, 11.

29 Francis Brown, Samuel R. Driver, and Charles A. Briggs, eds., *The New Brown-Driver-Briggs-Gesenius Hebrew-English Lexicon* (Peabody, MA: Hendrickson Publishers, 1979), 1006.

30 John D. W. Watts, John Joseph Owens, and Marvin E. Tate Jr., "Job," *The Broadman Bible Commentary*, ed. Clifton J. Allen, vol. 4 (Nashville: Broadman Press, 1972), 41.

31 Norman C. Habel, *The Book of Job*, The Old Testament Library, ed. Peter Ackroyd, James Barr, Bernhard W. Anderson, and James L. Mays (Philadelphia: The Westminster Press, 1985), 95.

32 Ibid.

33 http://www.apa.org/helpcenter/pain-management.aspx, accessed August 13, 2018.

34 https://www.psychiatry.org/patients-families/somatic-symptom-disorder/what-is-somatic-symptom-disorder, accessed August 13, 2018.

35 John E. Hartley, *The Book of Job*, The New International Commentary on the Old Testament, ed. R. K. Harrison (Grand Rapids, MI: William B. Eerdmans Publishing Company, 1988), 82.

36 "Dan & Hazel Hall: Hearts Set on the Journey," *Mississippi Christian Living* 12, no. 5 (November 2017): 35.

37 https://www.thegospelcoalition.org/blogs/justin-taylor/ nabeel-qureshi-1983-2017, accessed July 5, 2018.

38 C. S. Lewis, *The Problem of Pain* (New York: The Macmillan Company, 1944), 81.

39 See also Ecclesiastes 3:16; 4:1–3; 5:8; 8:10–11, 14; 9:1, 13–16; 10:5–7.

40 Fisher Humphreys, *The Nature of God* (Nashville: Broadman Press, 1985), 125.

41 Fisher Humphreys, *Thinking About God* (New Orleans: Insight Press, 1974), 119.

42 Leonard J. Coppes, *"nud," Theological Wordbook of the Old Testament*, vol. II, ed. R. Laird Harris (Chicago: Moody Press, 1980), 560–61; Hereafter cited as *TWOT*; H. W. F. Gesenius, *Gesenius' Hebrew-Chaldee Lexicon to the Old Testament* (Grand Rapids, MI: Baker Book House, 1979), 538.

43 Marvin R. Wilson, *"nacham," TWOT*, vol. II, 570.

44 Harold S. Kushner, *When Bad Things Happen to Good People* (New York: Schocken Books, 1981), 89.

45 Dinah Maria Craik, *A Life for a Life* (New York: Harper & Brothers, 1859), 169.

46 William M. Joel, "Honesty," recorded 1978, on *52nd Street*, Columbia.

47 Harold Louis Ginsberg, "Job the Patient and Job the Impatient," in *Congress Volume: Rome*, Supplements to Vetus Testamentum, vol. 17 (Leiden: E. J. Brill, 1969), 88–111.

48 Marvin H. Pope, *Job*, The Anchor Bible, ed. William Foxwell Albright and David Noel Freedman (Garden City, NY: Doubleday & Company, Inc., 1965), xxi–xxii.

49 https://www.britannica.com/topic/Occams-razor, accessed August 14, 2018.

50 Gordon D. Fee and Douglas Stuart, *How to Read the Bible for All Its Worth*, 2d ed. (Grand Rapids: Zondervan Publishing House, 1993), 194.

51 Philip Yancey, *Disappointment with God: Three Questions No One Asks Aloud* (Grand Rapids: Zondervan Publishing House, 1988), 235.

52 Carney and Long, 98.

53 R. Allan Culpepper, *Anatomy of the Fourth Gospel: A Study in Literary Design* (Philadelphia: Fortress Press, 1987), 16.

54 Carney and Long, 63.

55 "Higher Purpose," *Baylor Magazine* 17, no. 1 (Fall 2018): 21.

56 https://www.smithsonianmag.com/arts-culture/sound-silence-surprise-hit-180957672, accessed May 2, 2019.

57 https://www.riaa.com/gold-platinum/?tab_active=default award&ar=Simon+%26+Garfunkel&ti=Sounds+of+Si-lence#search_section, accessed May 2, 2019.

58 See also Psalms 28:1–2; 35:17–26; 39:7–13; 102:1–11; 109:1–5.

59 See also Job 9:3; 10:2; 13:6, 8; 23:6; 31:35.

60 Yancey, *Disappointment with God: Three Questions No One Asks Aloud*, 204.

61 Millard J. Erickson, *Christian Theology* (Grand Rapids, MI: Baker Book House, 1996), 266–67.

62 https://www.thesun.couk/news/6589507/edward-snowden-girlfriend-secrets-leak, accessed June 7, 2019; https://www.alja zeera.com/news/2017/05/nsa-spied-millions-commu nications-2016-170503080336520.html, accessed June 7, 2019.

63 https://www.aclu.org/blog/national-security/privacy-and-surveillance/nsa-continues-violate-americans-internet-privacy, accessed June 7, 2019.

64 See Genesis 50:20; Job 36:24–37:13; Psalm 104:14–17; Matthew 5:45; Romans 8:28; 1 Corinthians 3:1–9.

65 Elie Wiesel, *Night*, trans. Marion Wiesel (New York: Hill and Wang, 2006), 64–65.

66 *Merriam Webster's Collegiate Dictionary*, 10th ed., s. v. "dogmatism."

67 Ibid., s. v. "pessimism."

68 Jack P. Lewis, *"gil,"* TWOT, vol. I, 159.

69 *The Greatest Showman*, dir. by Michael Gracey (2017; 20th Century Fox, 2018 dvd).

70 Gerald C. Davison and John M. Neale, *Abnormal Psychology: An Experimental Clinical Approach*, 3rd ed. (New York: John Wiley & Sons, Inc., 1982), 416.

71 *Merriam Webster's Collegiate Dictionary*, s. v. "paranoia."

72 *Baton Rouge The Advocate*, 31 March 1995, p. 1 (E).

73 *Peter's Quotations: Ideas for our Time*, 144.

74 Fritz Rienecker, *Linguistic Key to the Greek New Testament*, ed. Cleon L. Rogers, Jr. (Grand Rapids, MI: Zondervan Publishing House, 1980), 755.

75 *Peter's Quotations: Ideas for our Time*, 144.

76 Ibid., 145.

77 Richard J. Foster, *Celebration of Discipline: The Path to Spiritual Growth* (New York: HarperOne, 1998), 7.

78 Yancey, *Disappointment with God: Three Questions No One Asks Aloud*, 201.

79 wordnetweb.princeton.edu/perl/webwn, accessed August 4, 2019.

80 David Mathis, *Habits of Grace: Enjoying Jesus through the Spiritual Disciplines* (Wheaton, IL: Crossway, 2016), 21.

81 https://www.lexico.com/en/explore/how-many-words-are-there-in-the-english-language, accessed August 15, 2019.

82 https://www.merriam-webster.com/help/faq-how-many-
    english-words, accessed August 15, 2019.

83 *Merriam Webster's Collegiate Dictionary*, s. v. "synonym."

84 *The New American Roget's College Thesaurus in Dictionary
    Form* (New York: Grosset & Dunlap, 1977), 212.

85 Louis Goldberg, "*hokma*," TWOT, vol. I, 283.

86 Derek Kidner, *The Wisdom of Proverbs, Job & Ecclesiastes*
    (Downers Grove, IL: Inter-Varsity Press, 1985), 142.

87 James L. Crenshaw, *Old Testament Wisdom: An Introduction*
    (Louisville: Westminster John Knox Press, 1998), 12.

88 Andrew Bowling, "*yir'a*," TWOT, vol. I, 401.

89 Gerhard von Rad, *Wisdom in Israel*, trans. James D. Martin
    (London: SCM Press LTD, 1972), 66.

90 William P. Brown, *Character in Crisis: A Fresh Approach to the
    Wisdom Literature of the Old Testament* (Grand Rapids, MI:
    William B. Eerdmans Publishing Company, 1996), 28.

91 https://www.thegraidenetwork.com/blog-all/2018/8/1/the-
    two-keys-to-quality-testing-reliability-and-validity, accessed
    September 17, 2019.

92 H. H. Rowley, *The Book of Job*, The New Century Bible
    Commentary, ed. Ronald E. Clements and Matthew Black
    (Grand Rapids, MI: William B. Eerdmans Publishing
    Company, 1983), 266.

93 Briscoe, 159.

94 Carney and Long, 159.

95 https://www.si. com/vault/2004/11/15/8191994/getting-
    by-on-146-mil, accessed November 7, 2019; https://
    www.cherrycollectables.com.au/blogs/cherry/12983857-
    throwback-thursday-latrell-spreewell, accessed November 7,
    2019.

96 *Merriam Webster's Collegiate Dictionary*, s. v. "self-esteem" and "self-worth."

97 Ronald B. Allen, "*apar*," TWOT, vol. II, 687.

98 http://www.datagenetics.com/blog/april12011, accessed May 13, 2020; https://www.thoughtco.com/worth-of-your-elements-3976054, accessed May 13, 2020.

99 Allen, *TWOT*, vol. II, 687.

100 David Kinnaman and Gabe Lyons, *Good Faith* (Grand Rapids, MI: Baker Books, 2016), 58.

101 https://www.nytimes.com/1988/02/22/us/swaggart-says-he-has-sinned-will-step-down.html, accessed June 3, 2020.

102 Bob George, *Classic Christianity* (Eugene, OR: Harvest House Publishers, 1989), 52.

103 Bart Millard, "I Can Only Imagine," recorded 1999, on *The Worship Project*, MercyMe Music.

104 *Merriam Webster's Collegiate Dictionary*, s. v. "prodigal."

105 Johnson Oatman, Jr., *Higher Ground*, 1892.

106 https://www.youtube.com/watch?v=DWfc2_pDZlU, accessed June 17, 2020; https://www.youtube.com/watch?v=-zJldv6jag0, accessed June 17, 2020.

107 Northrop Frye, *The Great Code: The Bible and Literature* (New York: Harcourt Brace Jovanovich, Publishers, 1982), 195.

108 *Merriam Webster's Collegiate Dictionary*, s. v. "comic relief."

109 https://www.softschools.com/examples/grammar/anticlimax_examples/152, accessed June 20, 2020; https://literarydevices.net/anti-climax, accessed June 20, 2020.

110 https://www.espn.com/nba/story/_/id/17246999/michael-jordan-famous-mike-gatorade-commercial-debuted-25-years-ago-monday, accessed June 25, 2020; https://www.cbssports.com/nba/news/be-like-mike-gatorade-remakes-

classic-michael-jordan-ad-with-zion-williamson-jayson-tatum-elena-delle-donne, accessed June 25, 2020.

111 https://www.poetryfoundation.org/poems/46550/the-new-colossus, accessed July 10, 2020.

112 https://www.history.com/news/patrick-henrys-liberty-or-death-speech-240-years-ago, accessed July 10, 2020.

113 https://www.nh.gov/almanac/emblem.htm, accessed July 10, 2020.

114 Pope, 268–76.

115 https://www.mentalfloss.com/article/55652/brief-history-jeopardy, accessed July 16, 2020; https://www.imdb.com/title/tt0159881, accessed July 16, 2020.

116 Charles Williams, *War in Heaven* (Grand Rapids, MI: William B. Eerdmans Publishing Company, 1949), 23–24.

117 Douglas Emory Loyd, "Patterns of Interrogative Rhetoric in the Speeches of the Book of Job" (PhD diss., University of Iowa, 1986), 2.

118 Walter Vogels, "The Spiritual Growth of Job: A Psychological Approach to the Book of Job," *Biblical Theological Bulletin* 11, no. 3 (July 1981): 78–80.

119 David Robertson, *The Old Testament and the Literary Critic* (Philadelphia: Fortress Press, 1977), 54.

120 Paul D. Duke, "Irony in the Fourth Gospel: The Shape and Function of a Literary Device" (PhD diss., The Southern Baptist Theological Seminary, 1982), 23.

121 See also John 11:49–52.

122 Robert Gordis, *The Book of Job* (New York City: The Jewish Theological Seminary of America, 1978), 465.

123 Randy Alcorn, *Heaven* (Carol Stream, IL: Tyndale House Publishers, Inc., 2004), 317.

124 James Dobson, *When God Doesn't Make Sense* (Wheaton, IL: Tyndale House Publishers, Inc., 1993), 9.

125 Gesenius, 281.

126 *An Essay on Criticism* 3.625.

127 Louis Goldberg, "*nᵉbala*," TWOT, vol. II, 547.

128 https://www.preceptaustin.org/annies_poems, accessed June 4, 2021.

129 Bob Goff, *Love Does* (Nashville: Nelson Books, 2012), 141.

130 Henry Ramsey Fowler, *The Little, Brown Handbook*, 2d ed. (Boston: Little, Brown and Company, Inc., 1983), 136.

131 Rowley, 266.

132 Hartley, 544.

133 Gary G. Cohen, "*shᵉbit*," TWOT, vol. II, 896.

134 Robert Gordis, *The Book of God and Man* (Chicago: University of Chicago Press, 1965), 4.

A free ebook edition is available with the purchase of this book.

To claim your free ebook edition:

1. Visit MorganJamesBOGO.com
2. Sign your name CLEARLY in the space
3. Complete the form and submit a photo of the entire copyright page
4. You or your friend can download the ebook to your preferred device

Print & Digital Together Forever.

Snap a photo   Free ebook   Read anywhere

CPSIA information can be obtained
at www.ICGtesting.com
Printed in the USA
JSHW080001081022
31438JS00001B/12

9 781631 958892